「意味順」英語表現トレーニングブック

Putting the Pieces Together:
Word Order in English
——The Workbook

著 石井洋佑 Yosuke Ishii
マイケル・マクドウェル Michael McDowell
監修 田地野彰 Akira Tajino

音声ファイルをダウンロード！

本書で紹介されている英文をネイティブが読み上げた音声を、
以下のサイトから無料でダウンロードしていただけます。
mp3 ファイルは、パソコン・タブレット・スマートフォンでご利用いただけます。

http://cloverpub.jp/go/imijun-english.htm

はじめに

「意味順」は京都大学名誉教授の田地野彰先生の考案による、面倒な文法用語一切抜きで英語のしくみの根幹である語順を説明する学習モデルです。現在では小学校から大学、社会人相手まで多くの教育の現場で使われています。このモデルの画期的ぶりは英語の本場のイギリスで「意味順」に基づいた英語教師向けの文法書が刊行されたことからも伺えます。「意味順」のモデルは下のように単純明快です。ことばを意味のかたまりごとに各スロットに放り込んでいくだけです。

例えば、「ゆうべジュリエットは自分の家の前でロミオにキスをしましたか？」なら

Magic Box	Who (What) だれ・なに	Does/Is する／です	Whom だれ	What/How なに・どんな	Where どこ	When いつ
Did	*Juliet*	*give*	*Romeo*	*a kiss*	*in front of her house*	*last night?*

How どのように	Why なぜ
passionately	*to show her love for him*

Magic Box はセンテンスのコミュニケーションの役割を変えるときに使います。言い切りのときは必要ないですが、ここではたずねる機能を与えるために Did が使われています。

Who(What) センテンスが話題にしている人・もの・ことがここにきます。

Does/Is Who(What) の動作を表わすことばがきます。状態を表わすときに後ろの Whom What/How につなぐための「…である」「…となる」という意味のことばがくることもあります。

Whom Does/Is にくる動作の受け手となる人がきます。

What/How にくる動作の受け手となるもの・ことがきます。Who(What) の状態を描写・説明することばがくることもあります。

Where 場所を表わすことばがきます。

When 時間を表わすことばがきます。

How 方法や手段を表わすことばがきます。必要なときにくるオプション扱いです。

Why 理由を表わすことばがきます。必要なときにくるオプション扱いです。

こうして、*Did Juliet give Romeo a kiss in front of her house last night?* という英語のセンテンスができあがります。

しかし、これだけ便利な「意味順」も説明を見てわかっただけではコミュニケーションには不十分です。「意味順」のことばの並びを耳で聴き、英文を口にし、書いてみるという知識を体得するステップが必要です。本書はそのトレーニングができるように、次のような構成になっています。

Noticing patterns ここでは各 Unit で身につけるべき表現のパターンを学習します。例文を目で見るだけでなく、音声を聴き、そして、文字をなぞって書いてください。音を聴くと、パッと意味が浮かぶようになるまで何度も聴くとよいでしょう。さらに、聴いた通りに英語を口から出す練習もしてください。

Weaving words [ ]のなかに / で分けられた語句を並び替えて、正しいセンテンスを作ってください。なるべく自力でやること。ただし、わからない語句は辞書で調べたり、できる人に訊いたりしてかまいません。また、前ページの Noticing patterns を見ても構いません。ただ、絶対に自分なりの答えを作るまで解答編は見ないでください。自分の答えを記入したら、その上で音声を聴きます。そして、もし、自分の答えが間違っていたら赤ペン（もちろん緑でも紫でも好きな色でどうぞ）で訂正します。１度で聴き取れなければ何度でも聴いてください。ここでどうしてもわからないときだけ、解答編で正解の英文をチェックしてください。そして、音声をモデルにして正しい英文を何度も口に出してください。

Practicing lines Noticing patterns Weaving words で学習した表現を含むダイアローグです。まずは何度も聴いて意味がわかるか確認してください。解答冊子には日本語訳が載っていますが、なるべくそれに頼らずに自力で聴いて英文がわかる境地に達することを目指してください（もちろん本当にわからない箇所は参照して構いません）。その際，学習した表現・気になった語句の発音などがあったらどんどんアンダーラインを引いたり、書き込みをしたりしてください。その後，音声の後を追うように声を出したり（シャドウイング）、一定の長さでポーズ（一時停止）をして、その部分だけをリピートしたり、ダイアローグの英文が必要あれば口をついて出てくるようになるまで練習してください。

本書に使われている英語の文法事項・表現はごく基本的なものです。でも、上の作業を実際やってみると結構辛いし、できないことに気づくはずです。実際、このレヴェルの英語をいつも口にできるような学習者はそれほど多くはありません。たぶん、このワークブックを仕上げたときにあなたはぐっと多くの学習者を追い抜いていることに気がつくでしょう。みなさんの学習がうまくいき、英語とより楽しく深く関わることができるようになることを祈っています。

Yosuke Ishii
Michael McDowell

目次

はじめに …… 2

UNIT 1 Where ～？（どこ…ですか？） …… 6

UNIT 2 Is there X ～？（X がありますか？） …… 8

UNIT 3 Here's X.（ここに X があります） …… 10

UNIT 4 This is X.（これ / こちらは X です） …… 12

UNIT 5 Are you ～？（あなたは…ですか？） …… 14

UNIT 6 Is X ～？（X は…ですか？） …… 16

UNIT 7 What's that? / What's this?（それ / これは何ですか？） …… 18

UNIT 8 Do you *do*?（あなたは…しますか？） …… 20

UNIT 9 Do you have X？（X をお持ちですか？） …… 22

UNIT 10 I don't *do* ～（私は…しない） …… 24

UNIT 11 Did you *do* ～？（…しましたか？） …… 26

UNIT 12 (Do you) like X?（X は好き（ですか？）） …… 28

UNIT 13 I like to *do* / I like *do*ing（…するのが好きです） …… 30

UNIT 14 What time ～？（何時に…？） …… 32

UNIT 15 When ～？（いつ…？） …… 34

UNIT 16 Who is X？（X は誰ですか？） …… 36

UNIT 17 How ～？（どうやって／どのように…？） …… 38

UNIT 18 How long ～？（どれくらいの長さ…？） …… 40

UNIT 19 How often do you *do*?（どれくらいの頻度で…しますか？） …… 42

UNIT 20 How many ～？（いくつ…？） …… 44

UNIT 21 How much ～？（いくら…？） …… 46

UNIT 22 What ～？（何…ですか？） …… 48

UNIT 23 What / How is X *do*ing?（X は何を／どうしていますか？） …… 50

UNIT 24 Are you going to *do*?（…する予定ですか？） …… 52

UNIT 25 Can you *do*?（あなたは…することができますか？） …… 54

UNIT 26 What do you *do*?（あなたは…しますか？） …… 56

UNIT 27 What ～ ? / What kind / type of ～ ?（どんな／何の…？）…… 58
UNIT 28 Could you *do*? / Can you *do*? / Would you *do*?（…していただけますか？）60
UNIT 29 I want you to *do*（私はあなたに…してほしい）…… 62
UNIT 30 Can I *do*? May I *do*?（…していいですか？）…… 64
UNIT 31 I'd like to *do* / I want to *do*（…したい）…… 66
UNIT 32 Do you want X?（X がほしいですか？）…… 68
UNIT 33 Do you want to *do*?（…したいですか？）…… 70
UNIT 34 Should I *do*?（…しましょうか？）…… 72
UNIT 35 Do you want me to *do*?（…しましょうか？）…… 74
UNIT 36 Let's *do*（…しましょう）…… 76
UNIT 37 Let me ～（私に…させてください）…… 78
UNIT 38 Do you know ～ ?（あなたは…を知っていますか？）…… 80
UNIT 39 How was X?（X はどうでしたか？）…… 82
UNIT 40 You have (got) to *do* / must *do* / should *do*（…しなければならない / …したほうがよい）…… 84
UNIT 41 You don't have to *do*（あなたは…する必要はない）…… 86
UNIT 42 Don't *do* / must not *do*（…するな / してはいけない）…… 88
UNIT 43 You can *do*（…してもよい）…… 90
UNIT 44 Why ～ ? — Because ～ ?（なぜ…？—…だからです）…… 92
UNIT 45 I don't know how to *do* / what to *do* / who to *do*（どうやって／何を／誰に…したらよいのかわからない）…… 94
UNIT 46 have / need X to *do*（…するための X がある／必要だ）…… 96
UNIT 47 You look ～（…のように見える）…… 98
UNIT 48 That's ～（それは…ですね）…… 100
UNIT 49 I think (that) ～（…だと思います）…… 102
UNIT 50 X told me (that) ～ / X said, "～"（X が…と言った）…… 104
Answer Key …… 106

UNIT 1

Where ～?

(どこ…ですか？)

Noticing patterns

001

バス停はどこですか？

あそこです

Magic Box	Who (What)	Does/Is	Whom	What/How	Where	When
Where is	*the bus stop?*					

Magic Box	Who (What)	Does/Is	Whom	What/How	Where	When
					Over there.	

どこに住んでいますか？

横浜です

Magic Box	Who (What)	Does/Is	Whom	What/How	Where	When
Where do	*you*	*live?*				

Magic Box	Who (What)	Does/Is	Whom	What/How	Where	When
					In Yokohama.	

いまどこにいますか？

銀行の前にいます

Magic Box	Who (What)	Does/Is	Whom	What/How	Where	When
Where are	*you*					*now?*

Magic Box	Who (What)	Does/Is	Whom	What/How	Where	When
					In front of the bank.	

Weaving words

002

1. [is / the bathroom / where] ? — Around the corner.

2. [can / trains / I / where / change] ? — At Ikebukuro.

3. [are / from / where / you] ? — I'm originally from Vancouver.

Practicing lines

003

Kevin: Excuse me, where is the bus stop?

Keiko: It's over there. In front of the bank.

Kevin: Oh, I see it. Thanks.

情報をたずねるセンテンスの作り方をマスターしてね！

Magic Box	Who (What)	Does/Is	Whom	What/How	Where	When
	The bus stop	*is*			*in front of the bank.*	

Magic Box	Who (What)	Does/Is	Whom	What/How	Where	When
	The bus stop	*is*			*where?*	

Magic Box	Who (What)	Does/Is	Whom	What/How	Where	When
Where is	*the bus stop?*					

UNIT 2

Is there X ～?

(X がありますか ?)

Noticing patterns　004

このあたりにコンビニエンスストアはありますか ?

Magic Box	Who (What)	Does/Is	Whom	What/How	Where	When
Is there	*a convenience store*				*around here?*	

冷蔵庫のなかに何か食べ物はありますか ?

Magic Box	Who (What)	Does/Is	Whom	What/How	Where	When
Is there	*any food*				*in the fridge?*	

このあたりにどこか食べるところはないですか ?

Magic Box	Who (What)	Does/Is	Whom	What/How	Where	When
Is there	*any place to eat around here?*					

Which	What kind?	What?	Why?
Any		*place*	*to eat around here*

Weaving words

005

1. [to the city / is / public transport / there / any] ? — Yes, there is the subway or the bus.

____

2. [the bus / on / a restroom / is / there] ? —Yes, there is. No problem.

____

3. [a / is / this / in / town / there / shopping mall] ? — No, you have to go to the next town.

____

Practicing lines

006

Kevin: Is there a convenience store around here? I want to get some snacks.

Keiko: Yeah, there are a few. One is over there. Another is next to the café. There's one on the corner too.

Kevin: Oh, there are so many!

この会話の a few, one, another, so many が
ちょっとよくわからない…

それはズバリ a few = a few convenience stores, one = one convenience store, another = another convenience store, so many = so many convenience stores ということだよ。

UNIT 3

Here's X.

（ここに X があります）

Noticing patterns

007

ここにあなたの鍵があります

Magic Box	Who (What)	Does/Is	Whom	What/How	Where	When
Here's	your key.					

これがお客様の切符（入場券）です

Magic Box	Who (What)	Does/Is	Whom	What/How	Where	When
Here's	your ticket.					

これがあなたの予定表です

Magic Box	Who (What)	Does/Is	Whom	What/How	Where	When
Here's	your schedule.					

Weaving words 🔊 008

1. [your / here's / receipt].

____

2. [change / your / here's].

____

3. [deal / the / here's].

____

Practicing lines 

Kevin: Hi, I have a reservation.

Clerk: May I have your name?

Kevin: Sure, my name is Kevin Burns.

Clerk: Okay. A single room for three nights, right? Here's your key.

ホテルのフロントでの会話。I have a reservation. / May I have your name? もよく使われる頻出フレーズ。

UNIT 4

This is X.

（これ／こちらは X です）

Noticing patterns

010

こちらはアンドリューさんです

Magic Box	Who (What)	Does/Is	Whom	What/How	Where	When
	This	is	Andrew.			

これが私の家です

Magic Box	Who (What)	Does/Is	Whom	What/How	Where	When
	This	is		my house.		

ここにいるのは私の夫です

Magic Box	Who (What)	Does/Is	Whom	What/How	Where	When
	This	is	my husband.			

これって上では紹介する人やものが単数だけど，複数のときはどうするのかな？

These are my kids.（ここにいるのは私の子供たちです）
These are my cars.（これらは私の車です）
みたいに These are ～. を使います。

Weaving words

011

1. [coworker / is / my / this], Andrew.

2. [car / is / my / this]. Please get in.

3. [table / is / this / your]. Please have a seat.

Practicing lines

012

Keiko : Kevin, this is Andrew. He's my friend.

Kevin : Hi Andrew. I'm Kevin. I'm from Vancouver. Nice to meet you.

Andrew : Nice to meet you, Kevin. I'm Canadian too. I'm from Toronto.

UNIT 5

Are you ～?

(あなたは…ですか？)

Noticing patterns

013

あなたは学生ですか？

Magic Box	Who (What)	Does/Is	Whom	What/How	Where	When
Are	you		a student?			

あなたはケイコさんのお友達ですか？

Magic Box	Who (What)	Does/Is	Whom	What/How	Where	When
Are	you		a friend of Keiko?			

(いま) 忙しいですか？

Magic Box	Who (What)	Does/Is	Whom	What/How	Where	When
Are	you			busy?		

Weaving words

014

1. [a tourist / you / are] ?

____

2. [you / tired / are] ?

____

3. [you / worker / office / an / are] ?

____

Practicing lines

015

Kevin: Keiko, are you a student?

Keiko: No, I'm an office worker. I work for an IT company.

Kevin: Oh, you are an office worker… but you're so young.

Keiko: You're very nice.

会社員は男性でも女性でも an office worker。日本語で OL と言うからといって女性会社員のことを *an office lady とか言ってはいけない。

UNIT 6

Is X ～?

(X は…ですか？)

Noticing patterns

016

アンドリューはあなたの彼氏ですか？

Magic Box	Who (What)	Does/Is	Whom	What/How	Where	When
Is	Andrew		your boyfriend?			

ブライアンはおとなしい人ですか？

Magic Box	Who (What)	Does/Is	Whom	What/How	Where	When
Is	Brian		a quiet person?			

ケイトは古いお友達ですか？

Magic Box	Who (What)	Does/Is	Whom	What/How	Where	When
Is	Kate		an old friend?			

Weaving words

017

1. [yours / car / this / is] ?

2. [is / trash / for / plastic bag / this] ?

3. [big / supermarket / the / is] ?

Practicing lines

018

Kevin: Is Andrew your boyfriend?

Keiko: No, he's just a friend.

Kevin: He's very nice.

Keiko: Right. He's also very smart. He knows a lot of things.

英語の smart は「頭がいい」ということ。イギリス英語なら clever がよく使われる。体型がやせているときは slim, slender で、デザインがおしゃれなときは stylish と言うんだ。

UNIT 7

What's that?/What's this?

（それ／これは何ですか？）

Noticing patterns

019

これは何ですか？　私のお守りです

Magic Box	Who (What)	Does/Is	Whom	What/How	Where	When
What's	this?					

Magic Box	Who (What)	Does/Is	Whom	What/How	Where	When
	It's			my lucky charm.		

これは何ですか？　私の芸術作品です

Magic Box	Who (What)	Does/Is	Whom	What/How	Where	When
What's	this?					

Magic Box	Who (What)	Does/Is	Whom	What/How	Where	When
	It's			my art work.		

これは何ですか？　オムレツです

Magic Box	Who (What)	Does/Is	Whom	What/How	Where	When
What's	this?					

Magic Box	Who (What)	Does/Is	Whom	What/How	Where	When
	It's			an omelet.		

Weaving words 020

1. [that / what's] ? — It's a penny whistle.

____

2. What's this? — [sandwich / a / it's].

____

3. What's that? — [car / my / it's / new].

____

Practicing lines  021

Kevin: What's this?

Keiko: Oh, it's my lucky charm.

Kevin: It looks cool. Where can I get one?

Keiko: I think you can get one at a shrine.

複数のものについて訊くときは
What are these?（これらは何ですか）
What are those?（それらは何ですか）

UNIT 8

Do you *do*?

（あなたは…しますか？）

Noticing patterns

022

あなたは新聞を読みますか？

Magic Box	Who (What)	Does/Is	Whom	What/How	Where	When
Do	you	ever read		the newspaper?		

あなたは職場に車で行きますか？

Magic Box	Who (What)	Does/Is	Whom	What/How	Where	When
Do	you	drive			to work?	

あなたは平日は早く起きますか？

Magic Box	Who (What)	Does/Is	Whom	What/How	Where	When
Do	you	get up				early on weekdays?

Weaving words

023

1. [at Uniqlo / ever / buy / do / you / clothes] ?

____

2. [sports / you / play / do / ever] ?

____

3. [work / you / do / part-time / weekends / on] ?

____

ever は Did you ever talk to Jenny?「ジェニーといままで話をしたことがありますか？」みたいに、過去からいまのことを問題にしているときに使われると思ったけど…

ever = at any time（どんなときでも）で、現在の習慣や未来のことをたずねるときにも使われる。

Practicing lines

024

Keiko: Do you ever read the newspaper?

Kevin: Yeah, I read it almost every day. How about you?

Keiko: Well, I seldom read the newspaper. I always check the news online.

UNIT 9

Do you have X?

(X をお持ちですか?)

Noticing patterns

025

車をお持ちですか？

Magic Box	Who (What)	Does/Is	Whom	What/How	Where	When
Do	you	have		a car?		

お子さんはいらっしゃいますか？

Magic Box	Who (What)	Does/Is	Whom	What/How	Where	When
Do	you	have	any kids?			

ここ、日本人の感覚的には *Do you have any kid? としたくなるけど、... any kids? としないとダメなんだ！

運転免許はお持ちですか？

Magic Box	Who (What)	Does/Is	Whom	What/How	Where	When
Do	you	have		a driver's license?		

Weaving words 026

1. [boyfriend / have / a / you / do] ?

2. [have / questions / you / any / do] ?

3. [secrets / do / any / you / have] ?

Practicing lines  027

Kevin: Do you have a car?

Keiko: No. I don't need a car. You can use trains to go anywhere in Tokyo.

Kevin: That's so true. Do you have a driver's license?

Keiko: Yes, I got my license a long time ago. Do you have a car, Kevin?

Kevin: Yes, I have a red sports car!

UNIT 10

I don't *do* ~

（私は…しない）

「自分は…しない」という習慣の否定。会話ではほとんど省略形しか使われないから、これらは全部覚えて間違えずに口から出るようにしてね。

I do not ➡ I don't
You do not ➡ You don't
He/She/It does not ➡ He/She/It doesn't
We do not ➡ We don't
They do not ➡ They don't

Noticing patterns

028

私はスカートははかない

Magic Box	Who (What)	Does/Is	Whom	What/How	Where	When
	I	*don't wear*		*a skirt.*		

私は生の魚は食べない

Magic Box	Who (What)	Does/Is	Whom	What/How	Where	When
	I	*don't eat*		*raw fish.*		

私はテレビは観ない

Magic Box	Who (What)	Does/Is	Whom	What/How	Where	When
	I	*don't watch*		*TV.*		

Weaving words

029

1. [gym / don't / the / go to / I].

____

2. [don't / him / very often / with / I / talk].

____

3. [every day / don't / to work / I / lunch / bring].

____

Practicing lines

030

Keiko: I don't wear a skirt. It is too girly.

Kevin: Well, I'm a guy, but I sometimes wear a skirt.

Keiko: Really?

Kevin: I wear a kilt and play bagpipes. It's a Scottish tradition. My mom was from Scotland.

Keiko: That's cool.

UNIT 11

Did you *do* ～?

(…しましたか?)

Noticing patterns

031

私のメール読んでくれた?

Magic Box	Who (What)	Does/Is	Whom	What/How	Where	When
Did	you	read		my e-mail?		

昨夜はよく眠れましたか?

Magic Box	Who (What)	Does/Is	Whom	What/How	Where	When
Did	you	sleep		well		last night?

あなたの上司と話をしましたか?

Magic Box	Who (What)	Does/Is	Whom	What/How	Where	When
Did	you	talk with	your boss?			

「人と話す」は talk with/to *whom* で必ず talk の後に with か to をつけるんだ。
*talk your boss とは言えないから注意しよう。

Weaving words ········ 032

1. [morning / the gym / go to / did / this / you] ?

____

2. [watch / did / soccer game / yesterday's / you] ?

____

3. [did / morning / see / you / this / Jessica] ?

____

Practicing lines ········  033

Keiko: Did you read my e-mail?

Kevin: Not yet. What's up?

Keiko: I have a business trip this weekend, so I can't go to the party on Saturday.

Kevin: No problem. Have a safe trip.

UNIT 12

(Do you) like X(?)

(X は好き（ですか？))

Noticing patterns

034

パスタは好きですか？

Magic Box	Who (What)	Does/Is	Whom	What/How	Where	When
Do	you	like		pasta?		

私はパスタが本当に好きです

Magic Box	Who (What)	Does/Is	Whom	What/How	Where	When
	I	really like		pasta.		

私はパスタは大嫌いです

Magic Box	Who (What)	Does/Is	Whom	What/How	Where	When
	I	hate		pasta.		

これを頭に入れておいてね。

I love X.
I really like X.
I like X.
I don't like X.
I don't like X at all.
I hate X.

好き ↕ 嫌い

Weaving words

035

1. [love / I / pasta]. I can eat it every day.

____

2. [spicy / like / I / really / foods]. Especially, I love curry.

____

3. [raw fish / like / don't / I]. Actually, I can't eat it.

____

Practicing lines

036

Kevin: Do you like Italian food?

Keiko: I love it. I like pasta and pizza. How about you?

Kevin: I don't like Italian food. I really like Chinese food.

Keiko: Oh, really? I can cook fried rice for you.

Kevin: Oh, please! I love fried rice.

UNIT 13

I like to *do* / I like *doing*

(…するのが好きです)

Noticing patterns 037

私はテレビでアニメを観るのが好きだ

Magic Box	Who (What)	Does/Is	Whom	What/How	Where	When
	I	like		to watch cartoons on TV.		

私はテレビでアニメを観るのが好きだ

Magic Box	Who (What)	Does/Is	Whom	What/How	Where	When
	I	like		watching cartoons on TV.		

私はテレビでアニメを観るのが好きじゃない

Magic Box	Who (What)	Does/Is	Whom	What/How	Where	When
	I	dislike		watching cartoons on TV.		

*I dislike to watch cartoons on TV. とは言えないの。love, like, hate は to *do*, *doing* の両方を後ろにとれるけど、dislike は *doing* だけ。

Weaving words

038

1. [weekends / I / tennis / like / on / playing]. It's good exercise.

   ____

2. [play / like / I / tennis / to]. It's fun.

   ____

3. [jogging / day / I / every / dislike]. I'm lazy.

   ____

Practicing lines

039

Kevin: I like watching cartoons on TV.

Keiko: Oh, I dislike watching cartoons. They are childish.

Kevin: Really? Some cartoons are really good.

Keiko: Well, they are good for kids. Why don't you watch the news? I like watching the BBC.

Kevin: Too boring! Too difficult!

UNIT 14

What time ～?

(何時に…?)

Noticing patterns

040

映画は何時に始まりますか？

Magic Box	Who (What)	Does/Is	Whom	What/How	Where	When
What time does	the movie	start?				

昨日の夜は何時に家に戻ってきたのですか？

Magic Box	Who (What)	Does/Is	Whom	What/How	Where	When
What time did	you	come			home	last night?

明日何時に待ち合わせしましょうか？

Magic Box	Who (What)	Does/Is	Whom	What/How	Where	When
What time should	we	meet up				tomorrow?

What time should we meet tomorrow? でもいいけど、知り合い同士が何かをするために待ち合わせるときは meet up のほうがよく使われる。meet だけだと「知らない人に初めて会う」っていうニュアンスが強いんだ。

Weaving words

041

1. [the / store / close / what time / does] ? — It closes at 8:00 P.M.

___

2. [what / wake up / you / time / this / did / morning] ? — I woke up around 7:30.

___

3. [usually / what / go to / time / do / bed / you] ?

___

Practicing lines

042

Keiko: What time does the movie start?

Kevin: At 6:00.

Keiko: It's 5:30. We still have half an hour. Let's go to the café over there.

Kevin: Sounds great.

UNIT 15

When ～?

(いつ…?)

Noticing patterns

043

いつ日本に来たのですか？

Magic Box	Who (What)	Does/Is	Whom	What/How	Where	When
When did	you	come			to Japan?	

いつその店は開いていますか？

Magic Box	Who (What)	Does/Is	Whom	What/How	Where	When
When is	the store			open?		

営業時間をたずねている。開店時間をたずねる
What time does the store open? との違いに注意。

旦那さんと初めて会ったのはいつですか？

Magic Box	Who (What)	Does/Is	Whom	What/How	Where	When
When did	you	meet	your husband			for the first time?

Weaving words

1. [working / when / here / you / did / start] ? — Seven years ago.

2. [are / for Germany / when / you / leaving] ? — Next Tuesday.

3. [sales meeting / when / the / is / next] ? — On the sixteenth.

Practicing lines

Keiko: When did you come to Japan?

Kevin: Five years ago.

Keiko: Do you like living here?

Kevin: Sure. I dislike natto, but except for that, I like everything.

except X, except for X は「X を除いて」という表現。The shop is open every day except Sunday. だと「その店は日曜日を除いて毎日営業している」。

UNIT 16

Who is X?

(X は誰ですか?)

Noticing patterns

046

リオネル・メッシとは誰のことですか？

Magic Box	Who (What)	Does/Is	Whom	What/How	Where	When
Who is	Lionel Messi?					

誰と付き合っているのですか？

Magic Box	Who (What)	Does/Is	Whom	What/How	Where	When
Who do	you	go out with?				

誰が明日スピーチをするのですか？

Magic Box	Who (What)	Does/Is	Whom	What/How	Where	When
	Who	is going to give		the speech		tomorrow?

Who は属性をたずねるときに使うんで、名前を訊くときには What's your name? / Can I have your name? で Who are you? とは言えないのね。それだと「あなたはいったい何者？」になっちゃう。

Weaving words

1. [over there / is / who / the lady] ? — She's Emily, Joe's new girlfriend.

____

2. [basketball / who / with / you / play / do] ? — Dan and Conrad.

____

3. [to / took / who / the / you / airport] ? — My sister did.

____

Practicing lines

Kevin: I like Lionel Messi. He's a super star.

Keiko: Who's Lionel Messi? I don't know him.

Kevin: Really? He's a soccer player from Argentina. Who is your favorite athlete?

Keiko: I love Kei Nishikori. He's a tennis player.

UNIT 17

How ～?

（どうやって／どのように … ?）

Noticing patterns

049

どのようにしてあなたはいつも職場に行くのですか？

Magic Box	Who (What)	Does/Is	Whom	What/How	Where	When
How do	you	usually get			to work?	

もう何回かでてきているけど、always, usually, often, sometimes, never とか頻度を表わす言葉は Does/Is の動作・行動を表わす言葉の前に入れるの。

渋谷駅にはここからどのように行けばよいですか？

Magic Box	Who (What)	Does/Is	Whom	What/How	Where	When
How do	I	get			to Shibuya Station from here?	

どのような形で連絡すればよいですか？

Magic Box	Who (What)	Does/Is	Whom	What/How	Where	When
How should	I	contact	you?			

Weaving words 050

1. [the event / how / I / about / find / can / information] ? — Go to the website.

2. [did / how / get to know / each other / you] ? — We met at a party.

3. [pronounce / how / word / you / this / do] ? — I say "behind."

Practicing lines 051

Keiko: How do you usually get to work?

Kevin: I ride my bicycle. It takes me about an hour.

Keiko: Even in winter?

Kevin: Of course! It makes me strong.

最後のセンテンスは Riding my bicycle to work makes me strong. という意味。「職場まで自転車で行くことが私を強くする」ということ。 make *whom* ～「人を～の状態にする」は p.61 にも出てくるけど、ぜひ覚えておこう。

UNIT 18

How long ～?

（どれくらいの長さ…?）

Noticing patterns

052

家から職場までどれくらいかかるのですか?

40分くらいです

Magic Box	Who (What)	Does/Is	Whom	What/How	Where	When
How long does	it	take	you		from home to work?	

Magic Box	Who (What)	Does/Is	Whom	What/How	Where	When
						About forty minutes.

毎日どれくらい電話を使うのですか？

約５時間です

Magic Box	Who (What)	Does/Is	Whom	What/How	Where	When
How long do	you	use		your phone		every day?

Magic Box	Who (What)	Does/Is	Whom	What/How	Where	When
						About five hours.

１日にどれくらい運動をしますか？

だいたい１時間半です

Magic Box	Who (What)	Does/Is	Whom	What/How	Where	When
How long do	you	exercise				a day?

Magic Box	Who (What)	Does/Is	Whom	What/How	Where	When
						About one and a half hours.

Weaving words 053

1. [it / long / from here / does / take / to the station / how] ? — About twenty minutes on foot.

____

2. [night / long / sleep / how / do / every / you] ? — About seven hours.

____

3. [you / Saturdays / work / how / do / on / long] ? — About eight hours.

____

Practicing lines  054

Kevin: How long does it take you from home to work?

Keiko: Well, probably one hour.

Kevin: It's very long.

Keiko: Right, but I can find a seat on the train most times, so I can read for the hour.

It takes *whom when*「人に時間がかかる」という表現はちょっと慣れるまで難しいかも。このセンテンスの頭の It が何を指しているのかというのは考えすぎないで、よく出てくるから覚えるようにしてね。簡単に言えば、What time is it?—It's 5 o'clock. のように時間を表わす it があるのだけど。

UNIT 19

How often do you *do*?

(どれくらいの頻度で…しますか？)

Noticing patterns

055

どれくらいの頻度でジムで運動をしますか？

Magic Box	Who (What)	Does/Is	Whom	What/How	Where	When
How often do	you	exercise			at the gym?	

どれくらいの頻度で映画を観に行きますか？

Magic Box	Who (What)	Does/Is	Whom	What/How	Where	When
How often do	you	go			to the movies?	

この go to the movies というのは go to a movie theater（映画館に行く）ということ。

あなたはどれくらいの頻度でお母さんに電話をしますか？

Magic Box	Who (What)	Does/Is	Whom	What/How	Where	When
How often do	you	call	your mom?			

Weaving words

056

1. [eat / how / do / often / pizza / you] ? — I eat it every week.

___

2. [often / do / haircut / you / a / get / how] ? — Once every two months.

___

3. [girlfriend / see / how / do / your / often / you] ?
— Probably once a week.

___

Practicing lines

057

Kevin: I go to the gym, but I still have a big stomach.

Keiko: How often do you exercise at the gym?

Kevin: Well, probably once a month.

Keiko: How often do you eat a cheeseburger?

Kevin: Almost every day.

UNIT 20

How many ~?

(いくつ…?)

Noticing patterns

058

1 日に何回食事をしますか？

Magic Box	Who (What)	Does/Is	Whom	What/How	Where	When
How many meals do	you	eat				a day?

切符（入場券）は何枚いりますか？

Magic Box	Who (What)	Does/Is	Whom	What/How	Where	When
How many tickets would	you	like?				

あなたは 1 週間に何時間働きますか？

Magic Box	Who (What)	Does/Is	Whom	What/How	Where	When
How many hours do	you	work				in a week?

Weaving words 059

1. [people / how many / there / in / are / your family] ? — Four people.

____

2. [brothers or sisters / do / many / you / how / have] ? — I have one brother and two sisters.

____

3. [New York / in / people / many / live / how] ? — About 8.6 million.

____

Practicing lines  060

Keiko: How many meals do you eat a day?

Kevin: Well, four or five times a day.

Keiko: Are you really on a diet?

Kevin: Yes, but I always feel hungry…

回数を表わす表現は once, twice, three times, four times, five times, ...というふうに言う。実は one time, two times という言い方は完全に間違いではないんだけど、once, twice のほうがより通りのいい表現なので、こちらを使うようにしよう。

UNIT 21

How much ~?

(いくら…?)

Noticing patterns

061

いくらほしいの？

Magic Box	Who (What)	Does/Is	Whom	What/How	Where	When
How much do	*you*	*want?*				

東京でアパート暮らしをするにはどれくらいのお金がかかりますか？

Magic Box	Who (What)	Does/Is	Whom	What/How	Where	When
How much does	*it*	*cost*		*to live in an apartment in Tokyo?*		

これはちょっと難しいかな。It costs *whom* how much「人に金額がかかる」という使い方をしてそれが金額をたずねるセンテンスになっているんだけど…

Magic Box	Who (What)	Does/Is	Whom	What/How	Where	When
	it	*costs*		*(90,000 yen)* *How much*		
	to live in an apartment in Tokyo					

手元にはどれだけのお金をお持ちですか？

Magic Box	Who (What)	Does/Is	Whom	What/How	Where	When
How much money do	*you*	*have*			*in your pocket?*	

Weaving words 062

1. [there / how / space / is / much] ? — There's a lot of space.

2. [in / much / drink / a week / you / how / do / coffee] ?
— About twenty cups of coffee, I think.

3. [how / you / at work / much / do / stress / have] ?
— I have a lot of stress.

Practicing lines  063

Keiko: Kevin, I hate to ask you this, but can I borrow some money?

Kevin: Sure. How much do you want?

Keiko: Just 1,000 yen.

Kevin: Here you are. How much money do you have in your pocket now?

Keiko: Nothing. I left my wallet at home. Anyways, thanks!

UNIT 22

What ～?

(何…ですか?)

Noticing patterns

064

何が起きたのですか?

Magic Box	Who (What)	Does/Is	Whom	What/How	Where	When
	What	happened?				

あなたはケヴィンの家で何をしたのですか?

Magic Box	Who (What)	Does/Is	Whom	What/How	Where	When
What did	you	do			at Kevin's house?	

あなたはゲイラに何を話したのですか?

Magic Box	Who (What)	Does/Is	Whom	What/How	Where	When
What did	you	tell	Gayla?			

それぞれ
An accident happened.
We played video games at Kevin's house.
I told Gayla everything.
のようなセンテンスの下線部がわからないと考えて。

Weaving words

065

1. [Gayla / did / to / what / say / you] ?
   — I just said "good luck!" to her.

2. [did / summer / during / what / do / the / you] ? — I went to Europe.

3. [today / you / did / what / for / lunch / eat] ?
   — A cheeseburger with onion rings.

Practicing lines

066

Keiko: Kevin, what happened? You're bleeding.

Kevin: I just stepped on a banana peel and fell to the ground.

Keiko: Wow. Unbelievable. You are like a character in a stupid comedy.

Kevin: Don't laugh, Keiko! Right … I was a bit careless then.

この You are like a character in a stupid comedy. の like は「好きである」じゃなくて､be like X で「X のようである」という使い方。似たような形に look like X(X のように見える、X に似ている) というのもよく使われるから覚えておこう。Karen looks like a super model. (カレンはスーパーモデルのように見える)

UNIT 23

What/How is X *doing*?

(X は何を / どうしていますか?)

Noticing patterns

067

あの女の子は何をしているのですか？

彼女は楽器を演奏しています

Magic Box	Who (What)	Does/Is	Whom	What/How	Where	When
What is	*the girl*	*doing?*				

Magic Box	Who (What)	Does/Is	Whom	What/How	Where	When
	She	*'s playing*		*an instrument.*		

最近何しているの？

車の運転を習っているんだ

Magic Box	Who (What)	Does/Is	Whom	What/How	Where	When
What are	*you*	*doing*				*these days?*

Magic Box	Who (What)	Does/Is	Whom	What/How	Where	When
	I	*'m learning*		*to drive.*		

調子はどう？

すこぶる順調だよ

Magic Box	Who (What)	Does/Is	Whom	What/How	Where	When
How are	*you*	*doing?*				

Magic Box	Who (What)	Does/Is	Whom	What/How	Where	When
				Pretty good.		

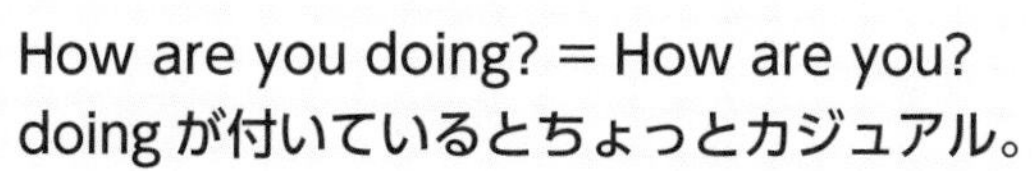

How are you doing? = How are you?
doing が付いているとちょっとカジュアル。

Weaving words

1. [doing / what / those / are / people] ? — They're performing a song.

____

2. [are / your / how / doing / parents] ? — They're doing well.

____

3. [you / weekend / doing / what / this / are] ? — I'm going to my son's soccer game on Saturday.

____

Practicing lines

Kevin: What is the girl doing?

Keiko: She's playing the guitar.

Kevin: I know that, but why is she performing on the street? It's cold outside.

Keiko: Well, she probably wants people to listen to her music, but she's not a pro yet.

Kevin: Oh, I feel sorry for her. I'll go give this 500-yen coin to the poor, pretty girl!

UNIT 24

Are you going to *do*?

(…する予定ですか？)

Noticing patterns

070

冬休みに帰省されるのですか？

Magic Box	Who (What)	Does/Is	Whom	What/How	Where	When
Are	you	going to go			back to your hometown	during the winter break?

クリスマスはご両親の家で過ごすのですか？

Magic Box	Who (What)	Does/Is	Whom	What/How	Where	When
Are	you	going to spend		Christmas	at your parents' place?	

明日はレストランで働くのですか？

Magic Box	Who (What)	Does/Is	Whom	What/How	Where	When
Are	you	going to work			at the restaurant	tomorrow?

is/are going to *do* = will *do* のように覚えている、教えられた、という人も多いけど、is/are going to *do* はあらかじめ決まっていること、will *do* はその場で決めたことや意志・推測を指すので、厳密には違うんだ。上の３つの例文も Will you ...? とするとちょっと変で、意味が変わってしまう。

Weaving words 071

1. [summer / you / anything / going to / are / do / this / special] ?
   — Yes, I'm going to surf in Hawaii.

   ____

2. [you / are / to / going / during / travel / the / around / vacation] ?
   — No, I'm going to stay home.

   ____

3. [tomorrow / going / a / you / to / are / give / presentation] ?
   — No, I'm just going to listen to others.

   ____

Practicing lines  072

Keiko: Are you going to go back to your hometown during the winter break?

Kevin: Not this time. I'm going back home in summer, though.

Keiko: Why aren't you going to go for Christmas?

Kevin: Because it's too cold in Vancouver in winter!

UNIT 25

Can you *do*?

（あなたは…することができますか？）

Noticing patterns

073

あなたは何か楽器を弾くことができますか？

Magic Box	Who (What)	Does/Is	Whom	What/How	Where	When
Can	*you*	*play*		*any musical instruments?*		

あなたはダンスをすることができますか？

Magic Box	Who (What)	Does/Is	Whom	What/How	Where	When
Can	*you*	*dance?*				

あなたの田舎では、スーパーに地下鉄で行くことができますか？

Magic Box	Who (What)	Does/Is	Whom	What/How	Where	When
Can	*you*	*take*		*a subway*	*to the supermarket in your hometown?*	

Weaving words 074

1. [computer / videos / you / can / edit / your / on] ? — Yes, I can.

2. [you / very / sing / can / well] ? — No, I'm a terrible singer.

3. [cook / can / fried rice / you] ? — Yes, of course. I'm a good cook.

Practicing lines 075

Kevin: Can you play any musical instruments, Keiko?

Keiko: Yes, I can play the violin. I started learning it a few years ago. How about you?

Kevin: I can play the guitar.

Keiko: Can you sing with the guitar?

Kevin: I could, but not anymore. I had a throat problem, and I can't sing loud now.

楽器を演奏するときは普通 <play ＋ the ＋ 楽器 > だけど、バンドとかのグループのメンバーがどの楽器を担当するというときは、Kenji plays guitar. のように <play ＋ 楽器 > になることもあるよ。

UNIT 26

What do you *do*?

(あなたは…しますか？)

Noticing patterns

076

仕事場には何を着て行きますか？

Magic Box	Who (What)	Does/Is	Whom	What/How	Where	When
What do	you	wear			to work?	

お仕事は何ですか（何をしてお金を稼いでいらっしゃいますか）？

Magic Box	Who (What)	Does/Is	Whom	What/How	Where	When	Why
What do	you	do					for a living?

暇なときは何をしていますか？

Magic Box	Who (What)	Does/Is	Whom	What/How	Where	When
What do	you	do				in your free time?

Weaving words 077

1. [do / do / on / you / weekends / what] ? — Just relax.

2. [eat / you / for / what / breakfast / do] ?
— A slice of toast and some eggs.

3. [do / you / study / what] ? — Physics.

Practicing lines 078

Kevin: What do you wear to work, Keiko?

Keiko: Like this. T-shirts and jeans.

Kevin: Really? I thought Japanese people wore formal clothes to work.

Keiko: Well, I work for an IT company. Everybody wears casual clothes.

上の Everybody wears casual clothes. を「みんな」だから複数と考えて、*Everybody wear ... とするのはありがちな間違い。

UNIT 27 What ～?/ What kind/type of ～?

(どんな / 何の…?)

Noticing patterns

079

あなたはどんな音楽を聴きますか？

Magic Box	Who (What)	Does/Is	Whom	What/How	Where	When
What kind of music do	you	listen to?				

あなたは何の映画を観たのですか？

Magic Box	Who (What)	Does/Is	Whom	What/How	Where	When
What movie did	you	watch?				

What movie(s) ～？には *Ferris Bueller's Day Off.* のように答えるのが普通。What kind of movies ～？だと Horror movies. のようにジャンルで答える。

あなたは何料理をよく食べますか？

Magic Box	Who (What)	Does/Is	Whom	What/How	Where	When
What foods do	you	often eat?				

Weaving words

080

1. [do / sports / what / play / you] ? — I sometimes play tennis.

2. [you / do / what type of / like / men] ? — I like caring men.

3. [topic / are / what / today / to / we / about / going / talk] ?
— Let's talk about last week's event.

Practicing lines

Kevin: What kind of music do you listen to?

Keiko: I often listen to rock music.

Kevin: Really? You play the violin, right?

Keiko: Well, I like performing classical music, but I like listening to rock music.

Kevin: I see. I like to play and listen to folk songs!

この会話には listen to X がたくさん出てくるけど，*listen rock music というように to を落とす人が本当に多いの。頭ではわかっているのかもしれないけど、自分が話すときにも間違えないように気をつけて！

UNIT 28 Could you *do*? / Can you *do*? / Would you *do*?

(…していただけますか？)

Noticing patterns

082

もう一度言っていただけますか？

Magic Box	Who (What)	Does/Is	Whom	What/How	Where	When
Could	you	say		that		again?

相手の言うことが聴き取れないときに使う。単に Excuse me? と言うことも多い。

後でメールをしてくれる？

Magic Box	Who (What)	Does/Is	Whom	What/How	Where	When
Can	you	send	me	an e-mail		later?

その塩を取っていただけますか？

Magic Box	Who (What)	Does/Is	Whom	What/How	Where	When
Would	you	pass	me	the salt?		

Weaving words

083

1. [give / could / a few / you / minutes / me] ? — Sure.

____

2. [that / you / repeat / can] ?
— Sure. "First, people should watch the movie and then judge it."

____

3. [a / the / door / you / second / hold / for / would] ? — No problem.

____

Practicing lines

084

Kevin: I made my wife angry last night.

Keiko: Could you say that again?

Kevin: I made my wife angry.

Keiko: Oh, I'm sorry. Why did she get angry?

Kevin: Well, she changed her hairstyle. It was very strange, so I laughed about it.

Keiko: Oh, poor Kevin. You can't laugh about your wife's hairstyle.

I made my wife angry. の make の使い方はちょっと難しいかも。
make *whom* ～で「人を～の状態にする」という意味。

UNIT 29

I want you to *do*

（私はあなたに…してほしい）

Noticing patterns

085

新しい彼氏に会ってほしい

Magic Box	Who (What)	Does/Is	Whom	What/How	Where	When
	I	*want*	*you*	*to meet my new boyfriend.*		

私の彼氏に対してやさしくしてほしい

Magic Box	Who (What)	Does/Is	Whom	What/How	Where	When
	I	*want*	*you*	*to be nice to my boyfriend.*		

『レッド・エプロン』で昼ごはんをごちそうしてほしい

Magic Box	Who (What)	Does/Is	Whom	What/How	Where	When
	I	*want*	*you*	*to buy me lunch at Red Apron.*		

このI want you to *do*は相手への希望・欲望をストレートに表現する言葉だから、くれぐれも目上の人や会ったばかりの人に使わないように。

Weaving words

086

1. [quiet / want / to / I / be / you].

____

2. [alcohol / stop / want / you / I / to / drinking].

____

3. [on Halloween / I / costume / you / sexy / to / a / wear / want].

____

Practicing lines

087

Keiko: I want you to meet my new boyfriend.

Kevin: You got a new boyfriend. Congrats! Sure, I can meet him. You're a wonderful girl, so he must be very handsome, rich, and smart!

Keiko: I want you to be quiet …

UNIT 30

Can I *do*? / May I *do*?

(…していいですか？)

Noticing patterns

088

何かお困りですか？

Magic Box	Who (What)	Does/Is	Whom	What/How	Where	When
May	I	help	you?			

失礼してよろしいですか？

Magic Box	Who (What)	Does/Is	Whom	What/How	Where	When
Can	I	leave				now?

leave には上の用法のほか、Michelle is leaving her job. のように去る対象を後ろにとる用法、Erica sometimes leaves her kids at her parents' place.（エリカはときどき両親のところに子供を預ける）のように「残す」「置いておく」という用法がある。

少しの間、席を外してよろしいでしょうか？

Magic Box	Who (What)	Does/Is	Whom	What/How	Where	When
May	I	excuse	myself			for a minute?

Weaving words 089

1. [Ms. Sander / speak / I / to / may] ?

____

2. [leave / can / message / I / a] ?

____

3. [photos / I / take / can] ?

____

Practicing lines 090

Clerk: May I help you?

Keiko: Yes, I'm looking for a coat.

Kevin: Let me show you some. … Here are the coats. Please have a look. If you have any questions, feel free to ask me.

Keiko: Will do. Thanks.

If you have any questions, feel free to ask me. はちょっと難しいかな。でも、If you have any X, feel free to *do*（Xがあれば、お気軽に…ください）は結構よく使われる。If you have any problems, feel free to contact us. のような決まり文句として使われるので、そのまま覚えていいと思う。

UNIT 31

I'd like to *do* / I want to *do*

(…したい)

Noticing patterns

091

これください

Magic Box	Who (What)	Does/Is	Whom	What/How	Where	When
	I	'd like to have		this.		

ローマに行ってみたい

Magic Box	Who (What)	Does/Is	Whom	What/How	Where	When
	I	want to visit		Rome.		

新しい車を買いたい

Magic Box	Who (What)	Does/Is	Whom	What/How	Where	When
	I	want to buy		a new car.		

日本語の「…したいと思う」の連想で、*I think I want to visit Rome.のように言う人が多いけど、このI thinkは要らない。だって、I would like to *do*, I want to *do* のなかに「思う」のニュアンスはすでに入っているから。

Weaving words ········ 092

1. There's a bug in my dish. [to / manager / speak / like / I'd / to the].

2. Do you want to have kids in the future? —Yes, [to / mother / I / be / a / want].

3. How would you like to pay? — [cash / I'd / to / pay / like].

Practicing lines ········  093

Keiko: Excuse me, I'd like to have this.

Clerk: Certainly. 80 dollars and 50 cents. How would you like to pay?

Keiko: Do you accept credit cards?

Clerk: Sorry, we accept some e-money, but not credit cards.

Keiko: That's okay. Then, I'll pay cash.

UNIT 32

Do you want X?

(X がほしいですか ?)

Noticing patterns

094

チョコレートほしいですか？

Magic Box	Who (What)	Does/Is	Whom	What/How	Where	When
Do	you	want		some chocolate?		

コーヒーほしいですか？

Magic Box	Who (What)	Does/Is	Whom	What/How	Where	When
Do	you	want		coffee?		

何か食べるものがほしいですか？

Magic Box	Who (What)	Does/Is	Whom	What/How	Where	When
Do	you	want		something to eat?		

もちろん、丁寧に言いたければ、Would you like X? も使えるよ。

Weaving words

095

1. [paper towels / want / do / some / you] ? — Sure, thanks.

____

2. [want / something / do / to / you / drink] ? — No, I'm good.

____

3. [you / candy / some / do / want] ?— No, thanks.

____

Practicing lines

096

Keiko: Do you want some chocolate?

Kevin: Sure. Yum-yum. This is really good. Where did you get it?

Keiko: I went to France for a business trip last week and bought it there.

Kevin: Cool.

UNIT 33

Do you want to *do*?

(…したいですか？)

Noticing patterns

097

ぼくの家で映画を観ない？

せっかくだけど，具合がよくないの

Magic Box	Who (What)	Does/Is	Whom	What/How	Where	When
Do	you	want to watch		a movie	at my place?	

Magic Box	Who (What)	Does/Is	Whom	What/How	Where	When
Sorry,	I	'm not feeling		well.		

あのトルコ料理の店で昼ご飯を食べようか？

うん、いいね

Magic Box	Who (What)	Does/Is	Whom	What/How	Where	When
Do	you	want to eat		lunch	at the Turkish restaurant?	

Magic Box	Who (What)	Does/Is	Whom	What/How	Where	When
Yeah,	that	sounds		great.		

明日買い物に行かない？

いいね！

Magic Box	Who (What)	Does/Is	Whom	What/How	Where	When
Do	you	want to go		shopping		tomorrow?

Magic Box	Who (What)	Does/Is	Whom	What/How	Where	When
		Sounds		good.		

Weaving words

🔊 098

1. [tonight / see / movie / do / to / want / a / you] ? — Sure.

____

2. [do / to / to / on / mall / you / go / want / the / Sunday] ?
— I'm sorry. I can't.

____

3. [play / on / want / you / to / tennis / Saturday / do] ?
— Sure, I'd love to.

____

Practicing lines

Kevin: Do you want to watch a movie at my place?

Keiko: I'm sorry. I'm not feeling well.

Kevin: Are you okay?

Keiko: I probably caught a cold. I'll go see a doctor tomorrow. Maybe next time.

Kevin: No problem. Keep warm and take care.

風邪を誰かからもらうことを catch a cold というけど、風邪をひいている状態は have a cold という。次の see a doctor とかもそうだけど、こういうよく使われるコロケーションを覚えることってセンテンスの組み立て方を覚えるのと同じくらい大事だよ。

UNIT 34

Should I *do*?

(…しましょうか？)

Noticing patterns

100

空港まで車でお送りしましょうか？

Magic Box	Who (What)	Does/Is	Whom	What/How	Where	When
Should	I	give	you	a ride	to the airport?	

何かお持ちしましょうか？

Magic Box	Who (What)	Does/Is	Whom	What/How	Where	When
Should	I	bring		anything?		

私からご主人に話してみましょうか？

Magic Box	Who (What)	Does/Is	Whom	What/How	Where	When
Should	I	talk to	your husband?			

相手のニーズを読んで、親切を申し出る場合、あるいは自分の判断が正しいのか相手にたずねる場合に使われるの。

Weaving words 101

1. [taxi / should / call / I / for / a / you] ? — Yes, please.

____

2. [give / chance / should / him / I / another] ? — No, you shouldn't.

____

3. [help / out / should / you / I] ? —Yes, thanks.

____

Practicing lines  102

Keiko: I'm leaving for France tomorrow.

Kevin: Oh, business trip again? Should I give you a ride to the airport?

Keiko: That'd be great. Is it okay?

Kevin: Sure. I'll pick you up at your place in the morning.

UNIT 35

Do you want me to *do*?

(…しましょうか？)

Noticing patterns

103

私が奥さんと話をしましょうか？

Magic Box	Who (What)	Does/Is	Whom	What/How	Where	When
Do	*you*	*want*	*me*	*to talk to your wife?*		

ちょっとだけアドヴァイスをしましょうか？

Magic Box	Who (What)	Does/Is	Whom	What/How	Where	When
Do	*you*	*want*	*me*	*to give you some advice?*		

家まで車で送りましょうか？

Magic Box	Who (What)	Does/Is	Whom	What/How	Where	When
Do	*you*	*want*	*me*	*to give you a ride home?*		

これも親切を進んで申し出るときの言い方。どちらかというとアメリカ英語らしい表現で、イギリス英語では Shall I *do*? がよく使われる。

Weaving words 104

1. [you / want / do / me / leave / to / alone / you] ?
   — Yes, I just need to think. Thanks.

   ____

2. [me / you / girlfriend / do / want / your / be / to] ?
   — Sorry, you're not my type.

   ____

3. [something / to / want / cook / you / for you / me / do] ?
   — Thanks. Actually, I'm starving.

   ____

Practicing lines  105

Kevin: My wife is really angry, but she doesn't tell me why. What should I do?

Keiko: Do you want me to talk to your wife?

Kevin: Would you? I don't understand women. Please help me out!

Keiko: Sure. I'll talk to her soon.

UNIT 36

Let's *do*

(…しましょう)

Noticing patterns 106

今週末にパーティーを開きましょう

Magic Box	Who (What)	Does/Is	Whom	What/How	Where	When
Let's		*have*		*a party*		*this weekend.*

小休憩を取りましょう

Magic Box	Who (What)	Does/Is	Whom	What/How	Where	When
Let's		*take*		*a short break.*		

家まで歩いて行きましょう

Magic Box	Who (What)	Does/Is	Whom	What/How	Where	When
Let's		*walk*			*home.*	

Weaving words

107

1. [go / let's / the movies / after work / to]. —Sounds like a good idea.

____

2. [invite / let's / Peter]. —Yeah, let's do it.

____

3. [Saturday / play / on / basketball / let's].
   — Sorry, my girlfriend is coming on that day.

____

Practicing lines

108

Kevin: Let's have a party this weekend. We can have a barbecue at my place.

Keiko: Sounds great. Who should we invite?

Kevin: Let's invite Peter, Michelle, and Annie. Oh, Andrew too.

Keiko: I will bring food and drinks.

Kevin: Awesome. Should be fun.

中学校の教科書では，Shall we *do*? という表現と一緒に学習することもあるが、Let's *do*. のほうが使用頻度がずっと高い。特にアメリカ英語では、一緒に食事をした後で席を立つときに「さあ行きましょうか」という感じでShall we? と使うほかは、あまり使われない。

UNIT 37

Let me ～

（私に…させてください）

Noticing patterns

109

飲み物を持ってくるよ

Magic Box	Who (What)	Does/Is	Whom	What/How	Where	When
		Let	me	get you a drink.		

ちょっと考えさせてください

Magic Box	Who (What)	Does/Is	Whom	What/How	Where	When
		Let	me	think		for a while.

仲間に入れてください

Magic Box	Who (What)	Does/Is	Whom	What/How	Where	When
		Let	me		in.	

Weaving words

110

1. [you / me / let / something / tell]. Rebecca is a liar.

____

2. [thoughts / your / let / know / me]. — Well, I think it's a good idea.

____

3. [my / let / calendar / check / me].... OK, I can join you guys.

____

Practicing lines

Keiko: Hey, Kevin. Wow, you live in a really nice house.

Kevin: Thank you. Have a seat. Let me get you a drink. What do you want?

Keiko: Just water would be fine.

Kevin: Sure. Excuse me for a second.

相手が断る可能性があるときは、Should I *do*? や Do you want me to *do*? が適切だけど、絶対断らないような場合は、Let me *do*. を使うのが自然。これは文法のルールというより、相手や状況に合わせて適切な表現を使う感じかな。

UNIT 38

Do you know ～?

(あなたは…を知っていますか？)

Noticing patterns

112

あなたはハルキ・ムラカミを知っていますか？

Magic Box	Who (What)	Does/Is	Whom	What/How	Where	When
Do	you	know	Haruki Murakami?			

明日が国民の祝日だと知っていますか？

Magic Box	Who (What)	Does/Is	Whom	What/How	Where	When
Do	you	know				

Magic Box	Who (What)	Does/Is	Whom	What/How	Where	When
(that)	tomorrow	is		a national holiday?		

この上の that は省略可能。

あなたは感謝祭を知っていますか？

Magic Box	Who (What)	Does/Is	Whom	What/How	Where	When
Do	you	know		Thanksgiving Day?		

Weaving words ································ 113

1. [brand of chocolate / you / know / do / this] ? — Yes, I love Godiva.

2. [Tak / a / do / guitarist / know / is / you / famous] ?
   — Of course, he's a rock star.

3. [you / that / a / do / know / got / Rachel / new boyfriend] ?
   — No, tell me about it.

Practicing lines ································  114

Keiko: Do you know Haruki Murakami?

Kevin: Yes, I actually just read his novel. The title was *Colorless Tsukuru Tazaki and his Years of Pilgrimage.* It was pretty good. It read like a mystery novel.

Keiko: Actually, I don't know that one. I read *Norwegian Wood* a long time ago.

Kevin: I like that one too.

UNIT 39

How was X?

(X はどうでしたか ?)

Noticing patterns

115

週末はどうだった？　少し退屈だった

Magic Box	Who (What)	Does/Is	Whom	What/How	Where	When
How was	your weekend?					

Magic Box	Who (What)	Does/Is	Whom	What/How	Where	When
	It	was		okay, a bit boring.		

映画はどうだった？　すごかった

Magic Box	Who (What)	Does/Is	Whom	What/How	Where	When
How was	the movie?					

Magic Box	Who (What)	Does/Is	Whom	What/How	Where	When
	It	was		amazing.		

テストはどうだった？　とても難しかった

Magic Box	Who (What)	Does/Is	Whom	What/How	Where	When
How was	the test?					

Magic Box	Who (What)	Does/Is	Whom	What/How	Where	When
	It	was		very difficult.		

Weaving words

116

1. [was / how / summer / your] ? — It was great.

____

2. [show / was / how / the] ? — It was exciting.

____

3. [Valentine's Day / was / how / your] ? — It wasn't very good.

____

Practicing lines

117

Kevin: How was your weekend?

Keiko: It was okay and a bit boring.

Kevin: Boring? You didn't go anywhere?

Keiko: My boyfriend got sick, and we canceled our plans to go to Kyoto.

Kevin: Oh, that's too bad.

How was your weekend? / How was your summer?
など、感想を求める言い方は、会話を切り出すときによく使われる。

UNIT 40 You have (got) to *do* / must *do* / should *do*

(…しなければならない／…したほうがよい)

Noticing patterns

118

奥さんと話をしないと

Magic Box	Who (What)	Does/Is	Whom	What/How	Where	When
	You	have to talk with	your wife.			

彼に本当のことを話さないといけないよ

Magic Box	Who (What)	Does/Is	Whom	What/How	Where	When
	You	've got to tell	him	the truth.		

I have a pen. が口語では I've got a pen. となるのと同じで、You have to tell him the truth. をこのように言える。もちろん Who (What) に Takako/She のような第三者がくるときは、Takako/She has got to tell her husband the truth. のように has got to *do* が使われる。

お医者さんに診てもらったほうがいいよ

Magic Box	Who (What)	Does/Is	Whom	What/How	Where	When
	You	should see		a doctor.		

Weaving words

119

1. [have / say / to / you / your girlfriend / to / sorry].
   — Why? I wasn't wrong.

____

2. [rule / follow / this / must / you]. — All right, boss.

____

3. I should lose weight. — [eat less / you / and / exercise more / should].

____

Practicing lines

120

Kevin: I made my wife mad again. I ate the cheesecake in the fridge. It was hers.

Keiko: Oh, you did a really bad thing. You've got to say sorry to her.

Kevin: I already did, but it didn't work.

Keiko: You should learn a lesson from this. You must not take other people's stuff.

Kevin: Right …

上の it didn't work はちょっと難しいかも。最初の it は I already did (= I already said sorry to her) を指しているけど、それがうまくいかないっていうこと。この work は「効果がある」という意味。

UNIT 41

You don't have to *do*

（あなたは…する必要はない）

Noticing patterns

121

明日は仕事をしなくていい

Magic Box	Who (What)	Does/Is	Whom	What/How	Where	When
	You	don't have to work				tomorrow.

今日、その報告書を終わらせる必要はない

Magic Box	Who (What)	Does/Is	Whom	What/How	Where	When
	You	don't have to finish		the report		today.

朝早く起きなくてもいいですよ

Magic Box	Who (What)	Does/Is	Whom	What/How	Where	When
	You	don't have to wake up				early in the morning.

理屈からすれば need to *do*（…する必要がある）を否定形にして you don't have to *do* として問題なさそうだけど、上から目線のニュアンスが出るので初級者は使わないほうが…。You'd better *do*（…するとまずい）を穏やかな助言には使わず may/might want to *do*（…するとよい）とすべきなのと同じく、社会規範の問題。

Weaving words 122

1. [don't / have / you / wear / to / here / a suit].

____

2. [sorry / be / have / you / to / don't].

____

3. [have / you / to / the / return / don't / money].

____

Practicing lines 123

Keiko: You look happy. What happened?

Kevin: I just found out that tomorrow is a national holiday. I don't have to work tomorrow.

Keiko: You don't like to work?

Kevin: No. We have to work hard, but we don't have to like our jobs.

このfind out that ～が「～ということに気づく」なのはちょっと難しいかな。thatの中にもう1つセンテンスが入っているわけだから。

UNIT 42

Don't *do* / must not *do*

(…するな／してはいけない)

Noticing patterns 124

それ以上言うな

Magic Box	Who (What)	Does/Is	Whom	What/How	Where	When
Don't		tell	me	more.		

バカなことはするな

Magic Box	Who (What)	Does/Is	Whom	What/How	Where	When
Don't		be		stupid.		

この写真をSNSに投稿してはいけません

Magic Box	Who (What)	Does/Is	Whom	What/How	Where	When
	You	must not post		this photo	on social media.	

Weaving words 125

1. Oh, you used my credit card! — Sorry, [get / mad / don't / me / at].

2. I can't sing in public. — [shy / be / don't].

3. Does Sara really like me? — [not / that / must / ask / you / her].

Practicing lines  126

Kevin: I talked with Andrew yesterday. He told me a really interesting thing.

Keiko: Don't tell me more.

Kevin: You were in a punk rock band. The band's name was *Strawberry Witches*. He gave me this photo. You had purple hair and green eyeshadow. So cool! Can I post it on social media?

Keiko: No, you must not do that! Don't ever show this picture to anybody else.

must *do* と have to *do* がどちらを「…しなければならない」という意味だからといって、その否定の形も同じ意味だと考えてはいけない。must not *do* は禁止、don't have to *do* は不必要を表わす。

UNIT 43

You can do

(…してもよい)

Noticing patterns

127

ここで写真を撮っても構いません

Magic Box	Who (What)	Does/Is	Whom	What/How	Where	When
	You	can take		photos	here.	

1つは無料で手に入れることができます

Magic Box	Who (What)	Does/Is	Whom	What/How	How	Where	When
	You	can get		one	for free.		

仕事を早く終わりにしていいですよ

Magic Box	Who (What)	Does/Is	Whom	What/How	Where	When
	You	can finish		work		early.

Weaving words 128

1. [can / bring / your / you / here / pet].

2. [online / can / you / tickets / buy].

3. [can / leave / early / today / you].

Practicing lines  129

Keiko: This is a really good museum. I can see a lot of nice art.

Kevin: Good. You can take photos here.

Keiko: Really? That's amazing. At most museums, you can't take photos.

Kevin: The creators of these works are still young, and people don't know them yet. They want us to help them become famous.

最後の They want us to help them become famous. はちょっと難しいかも。help *whom do* は「人が…するのを手助けする、手伝う」ということ。

UNIT 44

Why ~? — Because ~?

(なぜ…? — …だからです)

Noticing patterns

130

なぜカナダではホッケーは人気があるの?

面白いからだよ

Magic Box	Who (What)	Does/Is	Whom	What/How	Where	When
Why is	hockey			so popular	in Canada?	

Magic Box	Who (What)	Does/Is	Whom	What/How	Where	When
Because	it	is		fun.		

なぜゲイラは怒っているの?

弟にお金を取られたからだよ

Magic Box	Who (What)	Does/Is	Whom	What/How	Where	When
Why is	Gayla			angry?		

Magic Box	Who (What)	Does/Is	Whom	What/How	Where	When
Because	her brother	took		her money.		

なぜ美術館は閉まっているの?

今日は日曜日だから

Magic Box	Who (What)	Does/Is	Whom	What/How	Where	When
Why is	the museum			closed		today?

Magic Box	Who (What)	Does/Is	Whom	What/How	Where	When
Because	today	is				Sunday.

Weaving words 131

1. Why is Satoshi popular among girls?
   — [he's / everybody / nice / to / because].

   ____

2. [is / why / mad / Tom] ? — Because his girlfriend left him.

   ____

3. [the / why / closed / today / is / store] ?
   — Because today is a national holiday.

   ____

Practicing lines  132

Keiko: I don't understand. Why is hockey so popular in Canada?

Kevin: Well, because it is fun.

Keiko: It's not. People in most other countries like different sports. Why?

Kevin: Because there are not so many hockey rinks in those countries!

厳しい先生だと Because there are not so many hockey rinks in those countries. は文法的に間違いであって、People in most other countries like different sports because there are not so many hockey rinks in those countries. が正しいと言うかもしれないけど、それは書き言葉のルール。話し言葉では Because ～. は単独で頻繁に使われる。

UNIT 45 I don't know how to *do* / what to *do* / who to *do*

(どうやって / 何を / 誰に…したらよいのかわからない)

Noticing patterns

133

私は何をしたらよいのかわからない

Magic Box	Who (What)	Does/Is	Whom	What/How	Where	When
	I	*don't know*		*what to do.*		

私は車の運転の仕方がわからない

Magic Box	Who (What)	Does/Is	Whom	What/How	Where	When
	I	*don't know*		*how to drive a car.*		

明日のテストのために何を勉強したらよいのかわからない

Magic Box	Who (What)	Does/Is	Whom	What/How	Where	When
	I	*don't know*		*what to study for the test tomorrow.*		

Weaving words

134

1. [ask for / know / don't / who / I / help / to].

____

2. [the / museum / know / get / I / how / don't / to / to].

____

3. [I / my car / know / park / where / don't / to].

____

Practicing lines

135

Keiko: Andrew told everybody my secret. Now even my coworkers know it. I don't know what to do.

Kevin: Is there any problem? You were in a punk rock band. That isn't bad at all.

Keiko: I just don't want everybody to know my old hairstyle and makeup. I don't know how to make them forget it.

Kevin: Well, I actually kind of like you with purple hair and green eyeshadow.

Keiko: Kevin! Just forget it!

I don't know how to make them forget it. の make them forget it の部分が難しいかな。これは make *whom do* で「人に…させる」という用法。基本的な単語は、いろいろ覚えなければいけないことが出てくるけど、がんばってね。

UNIT 46

have/need X to *do*

(…するためのXがある / 必要だ)

Noticing patterns

136

話があるんだ

Magic Box	Who (What)	Does/Is	Whom	What/How	Where	When
	I	*have*		*something to tell you.*		

話し相手が必要なんだ

Magic Box	Who (What)	Does/Is	Whom	What/How	Where	When
	I	*need*	*somebody to talk to.*			

私はその件については何も関係がない

Magic Box	Who (What)	Does/Is	Whom	What/How	Where	When
	I	*have*		*nothing to do with the matter.*		

Weaving words 137

1. I can't decide right now. [need / I / think / time / to].

2. I am a writer. [I / a / alone / place / need / to / be].

3. I'm very busy. [a couple of / I / do / have / things / to]

Practicing lines 138

Kevin: I have something to tell you, Keiko.

Keiko: What's up, Kevin? I know you love me, but I have a boyfriend.

Kevin: You have a good sense of humor. I am thinking of forming a band. I need somebody to play music with.

Keiko: Are you asking me to be a member of your band? Well, I need time to think. Give me a few days.

Are you asking me to be a member of your band? が難しいかな。ask whom to *do*「人に ... することを頼む」という言い方。Mr. Quinn asked his assistant to organize files.「クインさんは秘書にファイルを整理するように頼んだ」

UNIT 47

You look ～

(…のように見える)

Noticing patterns

139

楽しそうですね

Magic Box	Who (What)	Does/Is	Whom	What/How	Where	When
	You	look		happy.		

お疲れのようですね

Magic Box	Who (What)	Does/Is	Whom	What/How	Where	When
	You	look		tired.		

お怒りのようですね

Magic Box	Who (What)	Does/Is	Whom	What/How	Where	When
	You	look		mad.		

Weaving words

140

1. [look / you / busy]. — Yes, I have a lot of things to do.

____

2. [great / look / you]. — Thanks.

____

3. [slim / look / you]. — Yes, I lost weight.

____

Practicing lines

141

Kevin: You look happy these days.

Keiko: Oh, really? Probably because I don't have any stress. I am enjoying my life.

Kevin: Good. Playing in a band is fun, right?

Keiko: Absolutely.

Kevin: How about dying your hair again?

Keiko: Stop saying that!

Magic Box	Who (What)	Does/Is	Whom	What/How	Where	When
	Playing in a band	*is*		*fun.*		

のような *doing* の用法も大事。最後の Stop saying that! を *Stop to say that! とはできない。「それをいうために立ち止まって」はここではおかしい。

UNIT 48

That's ～

(それは…ですね)

Noticing patterns 142

それはおかしい

Magic Box	Who (What)	Does/Is	Whom	What/How	Where	When
	That	's		crazy.		

それは不可能だ

Magic Box	Who (What)	Does/Is	Whom	What/How	Where	When
	That	's		impossible.		

それは不公平だ

Magic Box	Who (What)	Does/Is	Whom	What/How	Where	When
	That	's		unfair.		

この That's ～. は前に述べられたことにコメントする言い方。センテンスの作り的には簡単だけれども、会話を広げる上で的確にコメントできる人はそう多くはない。

Weaving words

143

1. I got a job. — [great / that's].

____

2. Gayla decided to become a dancer. — [interesting / that's].

____

3. My husband stepped on a banana peel and fell to the ground. — [funny / that's].

____

Practicing lines

144

Kevin: Let's hold a concert in Yokohama Arena.

Keiko: That's crazy. We can't do that.

Kevin: I was just kidding. Let's perform at a live house around here.

Keiko: That's great.

UNIT 49

I think (that) ~

（…だと思います）

Noticing patterns

145

私はあなたは正しいことをしたと思いますよ

Magic Box	Who (What)	Does/Is	Whom	What/How	Where	When
	I	think				

Magic Box	Who (What)	Does/Is	Whom	What/How	Where	When
that	you	did		the right thing.		

アンドリューは私のことが好きなんだと思う

Magic Box	Who (What)	Does/Is	Whom	What/How	Where	When
	I	think				

Magic Box	Who (What)	Does/Is	Whom	What/How	Where	When
(that)	Andrew	likes		me.		

ここの Magic Box に入る that は省略できるの。

まもなく雨が降ると思う

Magic Box	Who (What)	Does/Is	Whom	What/How	Where	When
	I	think				

Magic Box	Who (What)	Does/Is	Whom	What/How	Where	When
that	it	will rain				soon.

Weaving words ········ 146

1. [that / for you / I / too small / think / is / this T-shirt].
   — Well, let me try it on first.

   ____

2. [Rodger / I / doesn't / think / me / like]. — I don't think that's true.

   ____

3. [my / I / is / lying / husband / think]. — Why do you think so?

   ____

Practicing lines ········  147

Kevin: Wow, Keiko! You finally dyed your hair purple again.

Keiko: Don't look at me too much. I feel embarrassed.

Kevin: I think that you did the right thing.

Keiko: Is that so? I saw Andrew yesterday. He looked at me in a strange manner.

Kevin: I think that he likes you with purple hair.

UNIT 50

X told me (that) ~/ X said, "~"

(X が…と言った)

Noticing patterns

148

アンドリューは私のことをとてもおしゃれだと言った

Magic Box	Who (What)	Does/Is	Whom	What/How	Where	When
	Andrew	told	me			

Magic Box	Who (What)	Does/Is	Whom	What/How	Where	When
that	I	was		very stylish.		

上の Magic Box の that は省略可能。上下のセンテンスが同じ内容を言っていることに注意してね。

アンドリューは「あなたはとてもおしゃれですね」と私に言った

Magic Box	Who (What)	Does/Is	Whom	What/How	Where	When
	Andrew	said	(to me),			

Magic Box	Who (What)	Does/Is	Whom	What/How	Where	When
	"you	're		very stylish."		

お医者さんは私に「もっと運動をしなさい」と言った

Magic Box	Who (What)	Does/Is	Whom	What/How	Where	When
	My doctor	told	me			

Magic Box	Who (What)	Does/Is	Whom	What/How	Where	When
that	I	had to exercise		more.		

Weaving words 149

1. [to / me / said / my doctor], "you [more / have / exercise / to]."

____

2. [told / was / me / my / that / boyfriend / wrong / I].

____

3. ["you're / boyfriend / my / said,] wrong."

____

Practicing lines  150

Keiko: Andrew told me that I was very stylish.

Kevin: I told you. He likes you. He loves funky women.

Keiko: Well, I have a boyfriend. He's a nice guy, but I don't love him romantically.

Kevin: Poor Andrew. Don't worry. I'll tell him that you have a boyfriend.

Keiko: Thanks. That helps.

Putting the Pieces Together: Word Order in English The Workbook Answer Key

UNIT 1 Weaving words

1. Where is the bathroom?—Around the corner. お手洗いはどこですか？—角をまがったところにあります。
2. Where can I change trains?—At Ikebukuro. どこで電車を乗り換えたらよいですか？—池袋で。
3. Where are you from?—I'm originally from Vancouver. どちらのご出身ですか？—ヴァンクーヴァーです。

Practicing lines

Kevin: Excuse me, where is the bus stop? ケヴィン：すみません、バス停はどこですか？
Keiko: It's over there. In front of the bank. ケイコ：あそこです。銀行の前です。
Kevin: Oh, I see it. Thanks. ケヴィン：ああ、見えます。ありがとう。

UNIT 2 Weaving words

1. Is there any public transport to the city?—Yes, there is the subway or the bus.
市内までの公共交通機関はありますか？—はい、地下鉄かバスが使えます。

2. Is there a restroom on the bus?—Yes, there is. No problem.
バスにお手洗いはありますか？—はい、ございます。ご安心ください。

3. Is there a shopping mall in this town?—No, you have to go to the next town.
この町にショッピングモールはありますか？—いいえ、隣町に行かなくてはいけません。

Practicing lines

Kevin: Is there a convenience store around here? I want to get some snacks.
Keiko: Yeah, there are a few. One is over there. Another is next to the café. There's one on the corner too.
Kevin: Oh, there are so many!

ケヴィン：このあたりにコンビニはあるかな？ 軽く食べるものがほしいんだ。
ケイコ：ええ、いくつか。あそこに１つ。カフェの横にもう１つ。角にも１つ。
ケヴィン：へえ、そんなにたくさんあるのですね。

UNIT 3 Weaving words

1. Here's your receipt. これがあなたの領収書です。
2. Here's your change. おつりです。
3. Here's the deal. こういう取引はどうだ。

Practicing lines

Kevin: Hi, I have a reservation. ケヴィン：こんにちは、予約しているものですが。
Clerk: May I have your name? フロント係：お名前をお伺いできますか？
Kevin: Sure, my name is Kevin Burns. ケヴィン：もちろん、ケヴィン・バーンズです。
Clerk: Okay. A single room for three nights, right? Here's your key.
フロント係：そうですね。シングルで３泊ですよね？ これがキーです。

UNIT 4 Weaving words

1. This is my coworker, Andrew. こちらは私の同僚のアンドリューです。
2. This is my car. Please get in. これが私の車です。どうぞお乗りください。
3. This is your table. Please have a seat. これがお客様のテーブルです。どうぞおかけください。

Practicing lines

Keiko: Kevin, this is Andrew. He's my friend.
Kevin: Hi Andrew. I'm Kevin. I'm from Vancouver. Nice to meet you.
Andrew: Nice to meet you, Kevin. I'm Canadian too. I'm from Toronto.

ケイコ：ケヴィン、こちらはアンドリュー。私の友達です。
ケヴィン：やあ、アンドリュー。私はケヴィンです。ヴァンクーヴァー出身です、よろしく。
アンドリュー：よろしく、ケヴィン。私もカナダ人ですが、トロント出身です。

UNIT 5 Weaving words

1. Are you a tourist? あなたは旅行者ですか？
2. Are you tired? あなたは疲れていますか？
3. Are you an office worker? あなたは会社員ですか？

Practicing lines

Kevin: Keiko, are you a student? ケヴィン：ケイコ、君は学生なの？
Keiko: No, I'm an office worker. I work for an IT company. ケイコ：いえ、会社員よ。IT 企業に勤めているの。
Kevin: Oh, you are an office worker... but you're so young. ケヴィン：へえ、会社員なんだ。でも、すごく若いね。
Keiko: You're very nice. ケイコ：あなたすごくいい人ね。

UNIT 6 Weaving words

1. Is this car yours? これはあなたの車ですか？
2. Is this plastic bag for trash? このビニール袋はゴミ用ですか？
3. Is the supermarket big? そのスーパーは大きいですか？

Practicing lines

Kevin: Is Andrew your boyfriend? ケヴィン：アンドリューは君の彼氏なの？
Keiko: No, he's just a friend. ケイコ：いえ、ただの友達よ。
Kevin: He's very nice. ケヴィン：彼はとてもいいやつだね。
Keiko: Right. He's also very smart. He knows a lot of things.
ケイコ：そう。それにとても頭がいいの。いろんなことを知っているの。

UNIT 7 Weaving words

1. What's that? —It's a penny whistle. それは何？—ペニー・ホイッスルだよ。
2. What's this? —It's a sandwich. これは何？—サンドイッチだよ。
3. What's that? —It's my new car. それは何？—これは私の新しい車だよ。

Practicing lines

Kevin: What's this? ケヴィン：これは何？
Keiko: Oh, it's my lucky charm. ケイコ：ああ、これは私のお守り。
Kevin: It looks cool. Where can I get one? ケヴィン：それ、いかすね。どこで手に入れられるの？
Keiko: I think you can get one at a shrine. ケイコ：たぶん、神社で手に入れられるんじゃないかな。

UNIT 8 Weaving words

1. Do you ever buy clothes at Uniqlo? ユニクロで服を買うことがある？
2. Do you ever play sports? スポーツをすることがある？
3. Do you work part-time on weekends? 週末にバイトをしますか？

Practicing lines

Keiko: Do you ever read the newspaper? ケイコ：新聞を読むの？
Kevin: Yeah, I read it almost every day. How about you? ケヴィン：うん、ほとんど毎日読むよ。君は？
Keiko: Well, I seldom read the newspaper. I always check the news online.
ケイコ：うーん、新聞はほとんど読まないかな。ニュースはいつもネットでチェックするの。

UNIT 9 Weaving words

1. Do you have a boyfriend? 彼氏はいるの？
2. Do you have any questions? 何か質問はありますか？
3. Do you have any secrets? 何か隠していることがあるの？

Practicing lines

Kevin: Do you have a car?
Keiko: No. I don't need a car. You can use trains to go anywhere in Tokyo.
Kevin: That's so true. Do you have a driver's license?

Keiko: Yes, I got my license a long time ago. Do you have a car, Kevin?
Kevin: Yes, I have a red sports car!

ケヴィン：車を持っている？
ケイコ：いいえ、車は必要ないの。東京ではどこへでも電車で行けるでしょ。
ケヴィン：それはそうだね。免許は持っている？
ケイコ：うん、ずっと前に取った。ケヴィン、あなたは車を持っているの？
ケヴィン：うん、赤いスポーツカーを持っているのさ。

UNIT 10 Weaving words

1. I don't go to the gym. 私はジムには通わない。
2. I don't talk with him very often. 私は彼とはあまり話さない。
3. I don't bring lunch to work every day. 私は職場に毎日弁当を持ってくるわけじゃない。

Practicing lines

Keiko: I don't wear a skirt. It is too girly.
Kevin: Well, I'm a guy, but I sometimes wear a skirt.

Keiko: Really?
Kevin: I wear a kilt and play bagpipes. It's a Scottish tradition. My mom was from Scotland.
Keiko: That's cool.

ケイコ：私はスカートははかないの。スカートっていかにも女子って感じで。
ケヴィン：そうかな。ぼくは男だけど、たまにスカートをはくよ。
ケイコ：本当に？
ケヴィン：キルトを着て、バグパイプを吹くんだ。これはスコットランドの伝統なんだ。ぼくの母はスコットランド出身なんだ。
ケイコ：すてきじゃない。

UNIT 11 Weaving words

1. Did you go to the gym this morning? 今朝、ジムに行った？
2. Did you watch yesterday's soccer game? 昨日のサッカーの試合を観た？
3. Did you see Jessica this morning? 今朝、ジェシカに会った？

Practicing lines

Keiko: Did you read my e-mail? ケイコ：私のメールを読んだ？
Kevin: Not yet. What's up? ケヴィン：まだだけど、何かあったの？
Keiko: I have a business trip this weekend, so I can't go to the party on Saturday. ケイコ：今週末に出張があるんで、土曜日のパーティーには行けないの。
Kevin: No problem. Have a safe trip. ケヴィン：問題ないよ。気をつけて。

UNIT 12 Weaving words

1. I love pasta. I can eat it every day. パスタが大好きなんだ。毎日でも食べられるよ。
2. I really like spicy foods. Especially, I love curry. 辛い食べ物が好き。特に、カレーは大好き。
3. I don't like raw fish. Actually, I can't eat it. 生魚は嫌いなんだ。というか、食べられない。

Practicing lines

Kevin: Do you like Italian food? ケヴィン：イタリア料理は好き？
Keiko: I love it. I like pasta and pizza. How about you? ケイコ：大好き。パスタとピザが好きなの。あなたは？
Kevin: I don't like Italian food. I really like Chinese food. ケヴィン：イタリア料理は好きじゃない。中華料理がとっても好きなんだ。
Keiko: Oh, really? I can cook fried rice for you. ケイコ：本当？　チャーハンをつくってあげるよ。
Kevin: Oh, please! I love fried rice. ケヴィン：え、ぜひ！　チャーハンは大好きなんだ。

UNIT 13 Weaving words

1. I like playing tennis on weekends. It's good exercise. 週末はテニスをするのが好きなんだ。いい運動だからね。
2. I like to play tennis. It's fun. テニスをするのが好きだ。楽しいから。
3. I dislike jogging every day. I'm lazy. ジョギングを毎日するのはいやだ。怠け者だから。

Practicing lines

Kevin: I like watching cartoons on TV.
Keiko: Oh, I dislike watching cartoons. They are childish.
Kevin: Really? Some cartoons are really good.

Keiko: Well, they are good for kids. Why don't you watch the news? I like watching the BBC.
Kevin: Too boring! Too difficult!

ケヴィン：アニメをテレビで観るのが好きなんだ。
ケイコ：へえ、私はアニメ観るの嫌い。子供っぽくて。
ケヴィン：そうかな。アニメの中にはすごくいいのもあるよ。
ケイコ：まあ、子供にはいいかもしれないけど。ニュースを見たら？　私は BBC を観るのが好きなの。
ケヴィン：退屈すぎるよ！　難しすぎる！

UNIT 14 Weaving words

1. What time does the store close? —It closes at 8:00 P.M. 店は何時に閉店するの？—８時閉店だよ。
2. What time did you wake up this morning? —I woke up around 7:30. 今朝は何時に起きましたか？—７時半です。
3. What time do you usually go to bed? たいてい何時に寝るの？

Practicing lines

Keiko: What time does the movie start? ケイコ：映画は何時に始まるの？
Kevin: At 6:00. ケヴィン：６時。
Keiko: It's 5:30. We still have half an hour. Let's go to the café over there. ケイコ：いま５時半。まだ 30 分ある。あそこの喫茶店に行こう。
Kevin: Sounds great. ケヴィン：いいね。

UNIT 15 Weaving words

1. When did you start working here? —Seven years ago. いつ、ここで勤めはじめたの？—７年前。
2. When are you leaving for Germany? —Next Tuesday. ドイツにいつ発つの？—来週の火曜日。
3. When is the next sales meeting? —On the sixteenth. 次の営業会議はいつ？—16 日。

Practicing lines

Keiko: When did you come to Japan? ケイコ：いつ日本に来たの？
Kevin: Five years ago. ケヴィン：５年前。
Keiko: Do you like living here? ケイコ：ここのくらしは気に入っているの？
Kevin: Sure. I dislike natto, but except for that, I like everything. ケヴィン：もちろん。納豆は嫌いだけど、それ以外は全部好きだ。

UNIT 16 Weaving words

1. Who is the lady over there? —She's Emily, Joe's new girlfriend. あそこにいる女性は誰かな？—彼女はエミリー、ジョーの新しい彼女だよ。
2. Who do you play basketball with? —Dan and Conrad. 誰とバスケットボールをするの？—ダンとコンラッドだよ。
3. Who took you to the airport? —My sister did. 誰が空港に君を連れて行ったの？—私の妹だよ。

Practicing lines

Kevin: I like Lionel Messi. He's a super star.
Keiko: Who's Lionel Messi? I don't know him.
Kevin: Really? He's a soccer player from Argentina. Who is your favorite athlete?
Keiko: I love Kei Nishikori. He's a tennis player.

ケヴィン：ぼくはリオネル・メッシが好きだ。彼はスーパースターだ。
ケイコ：リオネル・メッシって誰？　そんな人、知らないけど。
ケヴィン：本当に？　彼はアルゼンチン出身のサッカー選手だよ。君の一番好きなスポーツ選手は誰？
ケイコ：ケイ・ニシコリかな。テニスの選手。

UNIT 17 Weaving words

1. How can I find information about the event? —Go to the website.
そのイベントの情報はどうやったら手に入れられるの？ — サイトに行くんだよ。

2. How did you get to know each other? —We met at a party.
あなたたちはどうやって知りあったの？— パーティーで会ったんだ。

3. How do you pronounce this word? —I say "behind."
この単語、どういうふうに発音するの？—「ビハインド」と自分は言うけど。

Practicing lines

Keiko: How do you usually get to work? ケイコ：どうやって仕事に行くの？

Kevin: I ride my bicycle. It takes me about an hour.
Keiko: Even in winter?
Kevin: Of course! It makes me strong.

ケヴィン：自転車で行くよ。1時間かかるんだ。
ケイコ：冬でも？
ケヴィン：もちろんだよ。鍛えられるんだ。

UNIT 18 Weaving words

1, How long does it take from here to the station? —About twenty minutes on foot.
ここから駅までどれくらいかかるの？—歩いて 20 分。

2. How long do you sleep every night? —About seven hours.
毎晩どれくらい睡眠をとるの？—だいたい7時間。

3. How long do you work on Saturdays? —About eight hours.
土曜日はどれくらい勤務するの？—だいたい8時間かな。

Practicing lines

Kevin: How long does it take you from home to work?
Keiko: Well, probably one hour.
Kevin: It's very long.
Keiko: Right, but I can find a seat on the train most times, so I can read for the hour.

ケヴィン：家から仕事場までどれくらいかかるの？
ケイコ：うーん、たぶん1時間くらいかな。
ケヴィン：かなり長いね。
ケイコ：そうね、でも、ほとんどの場合は電車で席に座れるから、その1時間で本が読める。

UNIT 19 Weaving words

1. How often do you eat pizza? —I eat it every week.
どれくらいの頻度でピザを食べるの？—毎週食べるかな。

2. How often do you get a haircut? —Once every two months.
どれくらいの頻度で髪を切りに行くの？—2か月に1回。

3. How often do you see your girlfriend? —Probably once a week.
どれくらいの頻度で彼女に会うの？—たぶん週1回。

Practicing lines

Kevin: I go to the gym, but I still have a big stomach.
Keiko: How often do you exercise at the gym?
Kevin: Well, probably once a month.
Keiko: How often do you eat a cheeseburger?
Kevin: Almost every day.

ケヴィン：ジムに通っているんだけど、まだお腹が出ている。
ケイコ：どれくらいの頻度でジムで運動するの？
ケヴィン：そうだなあ、月に一度かな。
ケイコ：どれくらいの頻度でチーズバーガーを食べるの？
ケヴィン：ほとんど毎日。

UNIT 20 Weaving words

1. How many people are there in your family? —Four people.
何人家族ですか？—4人家族です。

2. How many brothers or sisters do you have? —I have one brother and two sisters.
何人きょうだいですか？—男のきょうだいが1人と女のきょうだいが2人です。

3. How many people live in New York? —About 8.6 million.
ニューヨークの人口は？—約 860 万人です。

Practicing lines

Keiko: How many meals do you eat a day?
Kevin: Well, four or five times a day.
Keiko: Are you really on a diet?
Kevin: Yes, but I always feel hungry...

ケイコ：1日何食食べるの？
ケヴィン：うーん、4回か5回かな。
ケイコ：本当にダイエット中なの？
ケヴィン：うん、でもいつもお腹が空くんだ。

UNIT 21 Weaving words

1. How much space is there? —There's a lot of space.
どれくらいのスペースがある？—たくさんのスペースがあるよ。

2. How much coffee do you drink in a week? —About twenty cups of coffee, I think.
1週間にどのくらいコーヒーを飲むの？—たぶん、20 杯くらいじゃないかな。

3. How much stress do you have at work? —I have a lot of stress.
職場のストレスはどれくらい？—すごくストレスを感じる。

Practicing lines

Keiko: Kevin, I hate to ask you this, but can I borrow some money?
Kevin: Sure. How much do you want?
Keiko: Just 1,000 yen.
Kevin: Here you are. How much money do you have in your pocket now?
Keiko: Nothing. I left my wallet at home. Anyways, thanks!

ケイコ：ケヴィン、こんなこと頼みたくないけど、お金を貸してくれない？
ケヴィン：もちろん、どれだけ要るの？
ケイコ：1000円だけでいいよ。
ケヴィン：ほら。いま手元にどれだけのお金があるの？
ケイコ：ゼロよ。家に財布を置いてきちゃったの。とにかくありがとう。

UNIT 22 Weaving words

1. What did you say to Gayla? —I just said "good luck!" to her.
ゲイラに何を言ったの？—ただ「幸運を祈る」と言っただけだよ。

2. What did you do during the summer? —I went to Europe.
夏の間に何をしたの？—ヨーロッパに行った。

3. What did you eat for lunch today? —A cheeseburger with onion rings.
今日昼に何を食べたの？—チーズバーガーとオニオンリング。

Practicing lines

Keiko: Kevin, what happened? You're bleeding.
Kevin: I just stepped on a banana peel and fell to the ground.
Keiko: Wow. Unbelievable. You are like a character in a stupid comedy.
Kevin: Don't laugh, Keiko! Right ... I was a bit careless then.

ケイコ：ケヴィン、何があったの。血が出てるじゃない？
ケヴィン：バナナの皮を踏んで、転んじゃったんだ。
ケイコ：うわあ、信じられない。バカなお笑いの役みたい。
ケヴィン：笑うなよ、ケイコ。そうだな、あのときはちょっと不注意だったな。

UNIT 23 Weaving words

1. What are those people doing? —They're performing a song.
あの人たちは何をしているの？—歌を演奏しているんだ。

2. How are your parents doing? —They're doing well.
ご両親の調子はどう？—元気でやっているよ。

3. What are you doing this weekend? —I'm going to my son's soccer game on Saturday.
今週末何をするの？—土曜日に息子のサッカーの試合に行くんだ。

Practicing lines

Kevin: What is the girl doing?
Keiko: She's playing the guitar.
Kevin: I know that, but why is she performing on the street? It's cold outside.
Keiko: Well, she probably wants people to listen to her music, but she's not a pro yet.
Kevin: Oh, I feel sorry for her. I'll go give this 500-yen coin to the poor, pretty girl!

ケヴィン：あの女の子は何をしているのかな？
ケイコ：ギターを弾いているんだよ。
ケヴィン：それはわかっているよ、でも、なぜ道で演奏しているんだろう。外は寒いっていうのに。
ケイコ：うーん、たぶん、みんなに自分の音楽を聴いてほしいけど、まだプロになっていないのよ。
ケヴィン：そうか、彼女がかわいそうだ。よし、あのかわいそうな、かわいい子にこの500円玉をあげに行ってくる。

UNIT 24 Weaving words

1. Are you going to do anything special this summer? —Yes, I'm going to surf in Hawaii.
この夏何か決まったことをするの？—うん、ハワイでサーフィンをするんだ。

2. Are you going to travel around during the vacation? —No, I'm going to stay home.
夏休みにどこに旅行するの？—いや、家にいるよ。

3. Are you going to give a presentation tomorrow? —No, I'm just going to listen to others.
明日、プレゼンをするの？—いや、ほかの人のプレゼンを聞きにいくだけだよ。

Practicing lines

Keiko: Are you going to go back to your hometown during the winter break?
Kevin: Not this time. I'm going back home in summer, though.
Keiko: Why aren't you going to go for Christmas?
Kevin: Because it's too cold in Vancouver in winter!

ケイコ：冬休みに故郷に帰るの？
ケヴィン：いや、今回は戻らない。でも、夏には帰るよ。
ケイコ：なんでクリスマスに行かないの？
ケヴィン：だって冬のヴァンクーヴァーは寒すぎるんだよ。

UNIT 25 Weaving words

1. Can you edit videos on your computer? —Yes, I can. コンピューターで映像の編集はできる？—できるよ。
2. Can you sing very well? —No, I'm a terrible singer. 歌をうまく歌える？—いや、ひどい音痴なんだ。
3. Can you cook fried rice? —Yes, of course. I'm a good cook. チャーハンを作れる？—もちろん、料理は得意なんだ。

Practicing lines

Kevin: Can you play any musical instruments, Keiko?
Keiko: Yes, I can play the violin. I started learning it a few years ago. How about you?
Kevin: I can play the guitar.
Keiko: Can you sing with the guitar?
Kevin: I could, but not anymore. I had a throat problem, and I can't sing loud now.

ケヴィン：ケイコ、何か楽器は演奏できるの？
ケイコ：うん、ヴァイオリンを弾ける。数年前にはじめたの。あなたは？
ケヴィン：ギターが弾ける。
ケイコ：弾きながら歌える？
ケヴィン：できたけど、もうだめ。喉を痛めてしまって、いまは大声で歌えないんだ。

UNIT 26 Weaving words

1. What do you do on weekends? —Just relax. 週末には何をしますか？—ただ、くつろぐだけです。
2. What do you eat for breakfast? —A slice of toast and some eggs. 朝、何を食べますか？—トーストと卵。
3. What do you study? —Physics. 何を勉強していますか？—物理。

Practicing lines

Kevin: What do you wear to work, Keiko?
Keiko: Like this. T-shirts and jeans.
Kevin: Really? I thought Japanese people wore formal clothes to work.
Keiko: Well, I work for an IT company. Everybody wears casual clothes.

ケヴィン：ケイコ、職場にはどんな服を着ていくの？
ケイコ：こんな感じ。T シャツとジーンズ。
ケヴィン：本当に？　日本人はフォーマルな服を仕事場で着ていると思っていたのに。
ケイコ：うーん、私は IT 企業に勤めているから。みんなカジュアルな服を着ているよ。

UNIT 27 Weaving words

1. What sports do you play? —I sometimes play tennis.
あなたは何のスポーツをしますか？—たまにテニスをします。

2. What type of men do you like? —I like caring men.
どんなタイプの男性が好みですか？—やさしい男の人が好きです。

3. What topic are we going to talk about today? —Let's talk about last week's event.
今日はどんなトピックを話しますか？—先週のイヴェントについて話そう。

Practicing lines

Kevin: What kind of music do you listen to?
Keiko: I often listen to rock music.
Kevin: Really? You play the violin, right?
Keiko: Well, I like performing classical music, but I like listening to rock music.
Kevin: I see. I like to play and listen to folk songs!

ケヴィン：どんな音楽が好きなの？
ケイコ：よくロックミュージックを聴くけど。

ケヴィン：本当に？　ヴァイオリンを弾くんだよね？
ケイコ：そうねえ、クラシック音楽を演奏するのが好きだけど、聴くのはロックが好きなの。
ケヴィン：なるほど。ぼくはフォークソングを弾くのも聴くのも好きなんだ。

UNIT 28 Weaving words

1. Could you give me a few minutes? —Sure.
ちょっと時間をいただけますか？—もちろん。

2. Can you repeat that? —Sure. "First, people should watch the movie and then judge it."
繰り返してもらえますか？—もちろん。「最初に人々は映画を観て、それから判断するべきだ」。

3. Would you hold the door for a second? —No problem.
ちょっとの間、ドアを押さえていてもらえませんか？—了解。

Practicing lines

Kevin: I made my wife angry last night.
Keiko: Could you say that again?
Kevin: I made my wife angry.
Keiko: Oh, I'm sorry. Why did she get angry?
Kevin: Well, she changed her hairstyle. It was very strange, so I laughed about it.
Keiko: Oh, poor Kevin. You can't laugh about your wife's hairstyle.
ケヴィン：昨晩、奥さんを怒らせてしまった。
ケイコ：え、もう 1 回言ってくれる？
ケヴィン：奥さんを怒らせた。
ケイコ：ああ、気の毒に。で、なんで彼女は怒ったの？
ケヴィン：うーん、髪型を変えたんだ。それがすごく変だったんで、笑ってしまった。
ケイコ：もう、だめなケヴィン。奥さんの髪型を笑うなんて最低。

UNIT 29 Weaving words

1. I want you to be quiet. 静かにしてほしい。
2. I want you to stop drinking alcohol. 君にお酒を飲むのをやめてもらいたいんだ。
3. I want you to wear a sexy costume on Halloween. ハロウィンでセクシーな衣装を着て欲しいな。

Practicing lines

Keiko: I want you to meet my new boyfriend.
Kevin: You got a new boyfriend. Congrats! Sure, I can meet him. You're a wonderful girl, so he must be very handsome, rich, and smart!
Keiko: I want you to be quiet ...
ケイコ：私の新しい彼氏に会ってほしいんだけど。
ケヴィン：新しい彼氏ができたんだ。おめでとう。もちろん、喜んで会うよ。君はすばらしい女性だから、その男はきっとすごくハンサムで、お金持ちで、頭がいいに違いない。
ケイコ：あなたちょっとだまっててくれる？

UNIT 30 Weaving words

1. May I speak to Ms. Sander? サンダーさんと話せますか？
2. Can I leave a message? 伝言を残していいですか？
3. Can I take photos? 写真を撮ってもいいですか？

Practicing lines

Clerk: May I help you?
Keiko: Yes, I'm looking for a coat.
Clerk: Let me show you some... Here are the coats. Please have a look. If you have any questions, feel free to ask me.
Keiko: Will do. Thanks.
店員：いらっしゃいませ。
ケイコ：コートをさがしているんですが。
店員：いくつかお見せしましょう。コートはこちらです。どうぞご覧ください。何か訊きたいことがあれば、遠慮なく私におたずねください。
ケイコ：そうします。ありがとう。

UNIT 31 Weaving words

1. There's a bug in my dish. I'd like to speak to the manager.
料理に虫が入っていたんだ。支配人と話がしたい。

2. Do you want to have kids in the future? —Yes, I want to be a mother.
将来子供がほしい？—うん、お母さんになりたいの。

3. How would you like to pay? —I'd like to pay cash.
支払い方法はどうされますか？—現金で支払います。

Practicing lines

Keiko: Excuse me, I'd like to have this.
Clerk: Certainly. 80 dollars and 50 cents. How would you like to pay?
Keiko: Do you accept credit cards?
Clerk: Sorry, we accept some e-money, but not credit cards.
Keiko: That's okay. Then, I'll pay cash.

ケイコ：すみません。これ欲しいんですが。
店員：かしこまりました。80 ドル 50 セントです。支払い方法はどうされますか？
ケイコ：クレジットカードは使えますか？
店員：すみません、電子マネーは受け付けるのですが、カードには対応してございません。
ケイコ：わかりました。それでは、現金で払います。

UNIT 32 Weaving words

1. Do you want some paper towels? —Sure, thanks. ペーパータオルは要りますか。—はい、ありがとうございます。
2. Do you want something to drink? —No, I'm good. 何かお飲みになりますか？—いいえ、結構です。
3. Do you want some candy? —No, thanks. キャンディーは要りますか？—いえ、結構です。

Practicing lines

Keiko: Do you want some chocolate?
Kevin: Sure. Yum-yum. This is really good. where did you get it?
Keiko: I went to France for a business trip last week and bought it there.
Kevin: Cool.

ケイコ：チョコレートは要りますか？
ケヴィン：もちろん。ああ、おいしい。これ、本当においしいね。どこで手に入れたの？
ケイコ：先週出張でフランスに行って、そこで買ったの。
ケヴィン：いいね。

UNIT 33 Weaving words

1. Do you want to see a movie tonight? —Sure. 今晩映画を見ない？—もちろん。
2. Do you want to go to the mall on Sunday? —I'm sorry. I can't. 日曜日にモールに行かない？—ごめんダメなの。
3. Do you want to play tennis on Saturday? —Sure, I'd love to. 土曜日にテニスをしない？—もちろん。喜んで。

Practicing lines

Kevin: Do you want to watch a movie at my place?
Keiko: I'm sorry. I'm not feeling well.
Kevin: Are you okay?
Keiko: I probably caught a cold. I'll go see a doctor tomorrow. Maybe next time.
Kevin: No problem. Keep warm and take care.

ケヴィン：ぼくの家で映画を見ない？
ケイコ：ごめん。気分がよくないの。
ケヴィン：大丈夫？
ケイコ：たぶん、風邪をこじらせたの。明日病院に行く。また今度。
ケヴィン：ぜんぜん大丈夫だよ。暖かくして、お大事にね。

UNIT 34 Weaving words

1. Should I call a taxi for you? —Yes, please. タクシーを呼びましょうか？—お願いします。
2. Should I give him another chance? —No, you shouldn't. 彼にもう一度チャンスをあげたほうがいいかな？—いや、あげないほうがいいよ。
3. Should I help you out? —Yes, thanks. 手を貸しましょうか？—はい、お願いします。

Practicing lines

Keiko: I'm leaving for France tomorrow.
Kevin: Oh, business trip again? Should I give you a ride to the airport?
Keiko: That'd be great. Is it okay?
Kevin: Sure. I'll pick you up at your place in the morning.

ケイコ：フランスに明日発つの。
ケヴィン：また出張？　空港まで車で送ろうか？
ケイコ：そうしてくれるとうれしいけど、いいの？
ケヴィン：もちろん。明日の朝、君の家に迎えに行くよ。

UNIT 35 Weaving words

1. Do you want me to leave you alone? —Yes, I just need to think. Thanks.
ひとりにしておこうか？—うん、考えたいの。ありがとう。

2. Do you want me to be your girlfriend? —Sorry, you're not my type.
彼女になってあげようか？—ごめん、君はタイプじゃないから。

3. Do you want me to cook something for you? —Thanks. Actually, I'm starving.
何か作ってあげましょうか？—ありがとう。実は腹ペコなんです。

Practicing lines

Kevin: My wife is really angry, but she doesn't tell me why. What should I do?
Keiko: Do you want me to talk to your wife?
Kevin: Would you? I don't understand women. Please help me out!
Keiko: Sure. I'll talk to her soon.

ケヴィン：奥さんが怒っているけど、理由を話してくれないんだ。どうしたらよいだろう？
ケイコ：奥さんと話してみようか？
ケヴィン：頼めるかな。女性の考えていることは理解できないんだ。助けてよ。
ケイコ：もちろん。すぐ彼女に話してみるね。

UNIT 36 Weaving words

1. Let's go to the movies after work. —Sounds like a good idea. 仕事の後に映画に行こうよ。—いいね。
2. Let's invite Peter. —Yeah, let's do it. ピーターを呼ぼう。—そうしよう。
3. Let's play basketball on Saturday. —Sorry, my girlfriend is coming on that day. 土曜日にバスケをしよう。—ごめん、その日は彼女が来るんだ。

Practicing lines

Kevin: Let's have a party this weekend. We can have a barbecue at my place.
Keiko: Sounds great. Who should we invite?
Kevin: Let's invite Peter, Michelle, and Annie. Oh, Andrew too.
Keiko: I will bring food and drinks.
Kevin: Awesome. Should be fun.

ケヴィン：今週末にパーティーを開こう。ぼくの家でバーベキューをしよう。
ケイコ：いいね。誰を呼ぼうか？
ケヴィン：ピーターとミシェルとアニーを呼ぼう。おっとアンドリューも。
ケイコ：食べ物や飲み物は私が持ってくるね。
ケヴィン：すばらしい。楽しくなるはずだ。

UNIT 37 Weaving words

1. Let me tell you something. Rebecca is a liar. ちょっと言わせてもらうけど。レベッカはうそつきよ。
2. Let me know your thoughts. —Well, I think it's a good idea. 考えを聞かせてよ。—そうだね、いい考えだと思うよ。
3. Let me check my calendar.... OK, I can join you guys. カレンダーをチェックさせてよ。うん、仲間に入れるよ。

Practicing lines

Keiko: Hey, Kevin. Wow, you live in a really nice house.
Kevin: Thank you. Have a seat. Let me get you a drink. What do you want?
Keiko: Just water would be fine.
Kevin: Sure. Excuse me for a second.

ケイコ：あら、ケヴィン。うわあ、すごくいい家に住んでいるのね。
ケヴィン：ありがとう。座ってよ。飲み物を持ってくる。何がほしい？

ケイコ：ただの水でいいよ。
ケヴィン：わかった。ちょっとだけ待っててね。

UNIT 38 Weaving words

1. Do you know this brand of chocolate? —Yes, I love Godiva.
このチョコレートのブランド知っている？—うん、ゴディバは大好き。

2. Do you know Tak is a famous guitarist. —Of course, he's a rock star.
タクが有名なギタリストだって知ってる？—もちろん、彼はスーパースターだ。

3. Do you know that Rachel got a new boyfriend. —No, tell me about it.
レイチェルに新しい彼氏ができたって知ってる？—いいや、それ聞かせてよ。

Practicing lines

Keiko: Do you know Haruki Murakami?
Kevin: Yes, I actually just read his novel. The title was *Colorless Tsukuru Tazaki and his Years of Pilgrimage*. It was pretty good. It read like a mystery novel.
Keiko: Actually, I don't know that one. I read *Norwegian Wood* a long time ago.
Kevin: I like that one too.

ケイコ：ハルキ・ムラカミを知っている？
ケヴィン：うん、実は彼の本を読んだばかりなんだ。『色彩を持たない多崎つくると、彼の巡礼の年』という題のもの。すごくよかった。推理小説のように読めた。
ケイコ：実は、その本知らないの。私はずっと昔に『ノルウェイの森』を読んだ。
ケヴィン：その本も好きだな。

UNIT 39 Weaving words

1. How was your summer? —It was great. 夏はどうだった？—よかった。
2. How was the show? —It was exciting. その番組はどうだった？—わくわくした。
3. How was your Valentine's Day? —It wasn't very good. ヴァレンタインはどうだった？—あんまりよくなかった。

Practicing lines

Kevin: How was your weekend? ケヴィン：週末はどうだった？
Keiko: It was okay and a bit boring. ケイコ：まあまあ、ちょっと退屈だった。
Kevin: Boring? You didn't go anywhere? ケヴィン：退屈？　どこにも行かなかったの？
Keiko: My boyfriend got sick, and we canceled our plans to go to Kyoto. ケイコ：彼氏が病気で、京都行きの計画をキャンセルしたの。
Kevin: Oh, that's too bad. ケヴィン：それは残念だね。

UNIT 40 Weaving words

1. You have to say sorry to your girlfriend. —Why? I wasn't wrong.
彼女に謝らないと。—なんで？ ぼくは間違ってなかったのに。

2. You must follow this rule. —All right, boss.
このルールは守らないと。—わかりましたよ。

3. I should lose weight. —You should eat less and exercise more.
やせないと。—食べる量を減らして、もっと運動をしたほうがいいよ。

Practicing lines

Kevin: I made my wife mad again. I ate the cheesecake in the fridge. It was hers.
Keiko: Oh, you did a really bad thing. You've got to say sorry to her.
Kevin: I already did, but it didn't work.
Keiko: You should learn a lesson from this. You must not take other people's stuff.
Kevin: Right...

ケヴィン：また奥さんを怒らせた。冷蔵庫のチーズケーキを食べちゃったんだ。彼女のだったのに。
ケイコ：ひどいことをしたのね。奥さんに謝らないと。
ケヴィン：すでにそうしたさ、でも効果がなかった。
ケイコ：このことから学ばないと。人のものを取っちゃダメなのよ。
ケヴィン：そうだね…。

UNIT 41 Weaving words

1. You don't have to wear a suit here. ここではスーツを着る必要はない。
2. You don't have to be sorry. 謝る（気の毒に思う）必要はない。

3. You don't have to return the money.　そのお金は返す必要はない。

Practicing lines

Keiko: You look happy. What happened?
Kevin: I just found out that tomorrow is a national holiday. I don't have to work tomorrow.
Keiko: You don't like to work?
Kevin: No. We have to work hard, but we don't have to like our jobs.

ケイコ：うれしそうね。何があったの？
ケヴィン：明日が祝日だと気づいたんだ。働かなくていい。
ケイコ：仕事が好きじゃないの？
ケヴィン：うん。一生懸命仕事はやらないといけないけど、仕事を好きになる必要はないよ。

UNIT 42　Weaving words

1. Oh, you used my credit card! —Sorry, don't get mad at me.　あなた私のクレジットカードを使ったの！—ごめん、怒らないでよ。
2. I can't sing in public. —Don't be shy.　人前でなんて歌えないよ。—照れるなよ。
3. Does Sara really like me? —You must not ask her that.　サラはぼくを本当に好きなのだろうか？—それ本人に訊いちゃダメよ。

Practicing lines

Kevin: I talked with Andrew yesterday. He told me a really interesting thing.
Keiko: Don't tell me more.
Kevin: You were in a punk rock band. The band's name was *Strawberry Witches.* He gave me this photo. You had purple hair and green eyeshadow. So cool! Can I post it on social media?
Keiko: No, you must not do that! Don't ever show this picture to anybody else.

ケヴィン：昨日アンドリューと話したんだ。彼はすごく面白いことを言っていた。
ケイコ：それ以上言わなくていいわ。
ケヴィン：パンクロックのバンドに入っていたんだよね。バンドの名前はストロベリー・ウィッチーズ。彼はぼくにこの写真をくれたんだ。紫の髪で緑のアイシャドー。すごくカッコいい！　これ SNS にあげていいかな？
ケイコ：ダメよ、絶対にそんなことだめ。この写真はほかの誰にも見せないで。

UNIT 43　Weaving words

1. You can bring your pet here.　ペットをここに連れてきても大丈夫です。
2. You can buy tickets online.　チケットはネットで買える。
3. You can leave early today.　今日は早退して構いません。

Practicing lines

Keiko: This is a really good museum. I can see a lot of nice art.
Kevin: Good. You can take photos here.
Keiko: Really? That's amazing. At most museums, you can't take photos.
Kevin: The creators of these works are still young, and people don't know them yet. They want us to help them become famous.

ケイコ：ここは本当にいい美術館ね。すてきな作品がたくさん見られる。
ケヴィン：よかった。ここでは写真を撮ってもいいんだよ。
ケイコ：本当？　すごい。たいていの美術館では、写真を撮っちゃいけないのに。
ケヴィン：この作品のクリエーターたちはまだ若くて、まだみんなに知られていないんだ。彼らはぼくらに、彼らが有名になるのを手助けしてほしいんだ。

UNIT 44　Weaving words

1. Why is Satoshi popular among girls? —Because he's nice to everybody.
なぜサトシは女の子たちに人気があるのかな？—それは誰にでもやさしいからだよ。

2. Why is Tom mad? —Because his girlfriend left him.
なんでトムは怒っているの？—彼女に振られたから。

3. Why is the store closed today? —Because today is a national holiday.
なぜ今日店は閉まっているのかな？—今日は国民の祝日だからだよ。

Practicing lines

Keiko: I don't understand. Why is hockey so popular in Canada?

Kevin: Well, because it is fun.
Keiko: It's not. People in most other countries like different sports. Why?
Kevin: Because there are not so many hockey rinks in those countries!

ケイコ：わからない。なぜホッケーはカナダでこんなに人気があるの？
ケヴィン：そうだなあ、それは楽しいから。
ケイコ：楽しくないよ。ほかの国の人たちは違うスポーツが好きでしょ。なぜ？
ケヴィン：それは他の国にはホッケーの競技場がそんなにないからだよ。

UNIT 45 Weaving words

1. I don't know who to ask for help. 私は誰に助けを求めてよいのかわからない。
2. I don't know how to get to the museum. 私は美術館にどうやって行くのか知らない。
3. I don't know where to park my car. どこに車を停めたらよいのかわからない。

Practicing lines

Keiko: Andrew told everybody my secret. Now even my coworkers know it. I don't know what to do.
Kevin: Is there any problem? You were in a punk rock band. That isn't bad at all.
Keiko: I just don't want everybody to know my old hairstyle and makeup. I don't know how to make them forget it.
Kevin: Well, I actually kind of like you with purple hair and green eyeshadow.
Keiko: Kevin! Just forget it!

ケイコ：アンドリューはみんなに私の秘密をばらしてしまった。いまは私の同僚さえ知っている。どうすりゃいいの。
ケヴィン：何が問題なのかな？　パンクロックバンドにいた。それって全然悪いことじゃないよ。
ケイコ：私はただみんなに私の昔の髪型とお化粧を知ってほしくないの。どうやって忘れさせたらいいのかわかんないし。
ケヴィン：いや、正直、紫の髪で緑のアイシャドーの君も結構好きだけどな。
ケイコ：やめてよ、ケヴィン！　いいから忘れて！

UNIT 46 Weaving words

1. I can't decide right now. I need time to think. いま決められないよ。時間が必要だ。
2. I am a writer. I need a place to be alone. 作家だから、ひとりになる場所が必要なんだ。
3. I'm very busy. I have a couple of things to do. 忙しいんだ。いくつかやらなきゃいけないことがあって。

Practicing lines

Kevin: I have something to tell you, Keiko.
Keiko: What's up, Kevin? I know you love me, but I have a boyfriend.
Kevin: You have a good sense of humor. I am thinking of forming a band. I need somebody to play music with.
Keiko: Are you asking me to be a member of your band? Well, I need time to think. Give me a few days.

ケヴィン：ケイコ、話があるんだ。
ケイコ：どうしたの、ケヴィン。私のことが好きなのはわかるけど、彼氏がいるんだからね。
ケヴィン：ユーモアのセンスがあるね。ぼくはバンドをつくろうと思っているんだ。誰か一緒にやれる人がいないかと思って。
ケイコ：私にメンバーになってと頼んでいるの？　うーん、考える時間が要るな。何日か待ってよ。

UNIT 47 Weaving words

1. You look busy. —Yes, I have a lot of things to do. 忙しそうだね。—うん、やることが山ほどあるの。
2. You look great. —Thanks. よく見えるよ。—ありがとう。
3. You look slim. —Yes, I lost weight. スリムに見えるよ。—そう、体重を減らしたの。

Practicing lines

Kevin: You look happy these days. ケヴィン：：最近、楽しそうだね。
Keiko: Oh, really? Probably because I don't have any stress. I am enjoying my life.
ケイコ:本当？ たぶん、ストレスが全然ないからじゃないかな。生活が楽しいの。
Kevin: Good. Playing in a band is fun, right? ケヴィン：よかった。バンドをやるって楽しいよね？
Keiko: Absolutely. ケイコ：まさに。
Kevin: How about dying your hair again? ケヴィン：また髪を染めてみるのはどうかな？
Keiko: Stop saying that! ケイコ：それ言うの、やめてよ！

UNIT 48 Weaving words

1. I got a job. —That's great.
仕事が見つかったんだ。—それはよかった。

2. Gayla decided to become a dancer. —That's interesting.
ゲイラはダンサーになるって決めたんだ。—それは面白い。

3. My husband stepped on a banana peel and fell to the ground yesterday.—That's funny.
夫が昨日バナナの皮を踏んで、転んじゃったの。—それは面白い。

Practicing lines

Kevin: Let's hold a concert in Yokohama Arena.
Keiko: That's crazy. We can't do that.
Kevin: I was just kidding. Let's perform at a live house around here.
Keiko: That's great.

ケヴィン：横浜アリーナでコンサートを開こう。
ケイコ：それはいかれてるわ。私たちにそれは無理よ。
ケヴィン：冗談だよ。このあたりのライヴハウスで演奏しようよ。
ケイコ：それはいいね。

UNIT 49 Weaving words

1. I think that this T-shirt is too small for you. —Well, let me try it on first.
このＴシャツはあなたには小さすぎると思う。—そうかな、まず試着させてよ。

2. I think Rodger doesn't like me. —I don't think that's true.
ロジャーは私のこと嫌いなんだと思う。そうとは思わないけど。

3. I think my husband is lying. —Why do you think so?
夫はうそついていると思う。—なんでそう思うの？

Practicing lines

Kevin: Wow, Keiko! You finally dyed your hair purple again.
Keiko: Don't look at me too much. I feel embarrassed.
Kevin: I think that you did the right thing.
Keiko: Is that so? I saw Andrew yesterday. He looked at me in a strange manner.
Kevin: I think that he likes you with purple hair.

ケヴィン：わあ、ケイコ！　ついに、髪の毛をまた紫色に染めたんだね。
ケイコ：あんまり見ないでちょうだい。はずかしい。
ケヴィン：たぶん正しいことをしたと思うよ。
ケイコ：そうかなあ、昨日アンドリューに会ったの。彼は私を変な目で見てたわ。
ケヴィン：彼は紫の髪の君が好きなんだと思うよ。

UNIT 50 Weaving words

1. My doctor said to me, "you have to exercise more." お医者さんは私に「もっと運動をしないといけない」と言った。
2. My boyfriend told me that I was wrong. 彼氏は私が間違っていると言った。
3. My boyfriend said, "you're wrong." 彼氏は「お前が間違っている」と言った。

Practicing lines

Keiko: Andrew told me that I was very stylish.
Kevin: I told you. He likes you. He loves funky women.
Keiko: Well, I have a boyfriend. He's a nice guy, but I don't love him romantically.
Kevin: Poor Andrew. Don't worry. I'll tell him that you have a boyfriend.
Keiko: Thanks. That helps.

ケイコ：アンドリューが私に、君はすごくおしゃれだな。と言ってきた。
ケヴィン：言っただろ。彼は君のことが好きなんだ。彼はファンキーな女の子が大好きだから。
ケイコ：うーん、でも私には彼氏がいるのに。彼はいい人だけど、恋愛の対象にはならないのよ。
ケヴィン：かわいそうなアンドリュー。心配ないよ。ぼくから彼に、君には彼氏がいると言っとくよ。
ケイコ：ありがとう。助かるわ。

著者

石井洋佑 *Yosuke Ishii*

セントラルミズーリ大学大学院で第2外国語のための英語教育（TESL）修士号を取得。外国語教材編集者、イリノイ州の公立高校教員、留学コーディネーター、企業研修コンサルタントなどを経験後、現在は教育機関や企業から仕事を請け負うかたわら、英語学習書の執筆に携わる。著書に『TOEIC LISTENING AND READING テスト　おまかせ 730 点！』（アルク）、『ネイティブなら小学生でも知っている会話の基本ルール』（テイエス企画）などがある。

マイケル・マクドウェル *Michael McDowell*

アリゾナ州出身。南カリフォルニア大学で国際関係学（東アジア）を学ぶ。2004 年の来日以来、英語教師として多様な学習者を指導する。2008 年以降は企業・医療機関・英語教材出版社の依頼で英文の作成・校正・リライトもしている。著書に『はじめての TOEIC L&R テスト きほんのきほん』（スリーエーネットワーク）、執筆協力に『合格への集中対策 TEAP 予想問題』（テイエス企画）などがある。趣味はアウトドアと文学作品鑑賞。

監修

田地野彰 *Akira Tajino*

名古屋外国語大学教授。京都大学名誉教授。言語学博士。ELT Journal（英国オックスフォードジャーナル）編集委員（2012 年－ 2015 年）。専門は教育言語学・英語教育で、英語のカリキュラムや教授法、学習法、教育文法、教材などの開発研究に取り組んでいる。

NHK Eテレ「基礎英語ミニ」(2012 年度上半期)の監修、およびNHK ラジオテキスト「基礎英語 1」(2013 年度、2014 年度)にて「あたらしい英語の教科書」の連載を担当。現在は、小学校から大学まで意味順を取り入れながら、幅広い視点から英語教育システム全体を見直す研究を行っている。おもな著書に『＜意味順＞英作文のすすめ』（岩波ジュニア新書）、『「意味順」英語学習法』（ディスカヴァー・トゥエンティワン）、『「意味順」で中学英語をやり直す本』（監修、KADOKAWA/中経出版）、『NHK 基礎英語 中学英語完全マスター「意味順」書き込み練習帳』(NHK 出版)、『(Σベスト)「意味順」ですっきりわかる高校基礎英語』（監修、文英堂）、『英語初心者もレベルアップ！「意味順」書き込み練習帳 日常英会話編』（NHK 出版）などがある。

ナレーター	J. P. Mudryj, Gayla Ishikawa
本文デザイン	一柳 茂（クリエーターズユニオン）
イラスト	Yuki Tateyama
装丁	panix [keiichi Nakanishi]
校正協力	大江奈保子

「意味順」英語表現トレーニングブック

初版1刷発行 ● 2020年9月23日

著者

石井（いしい） 洋佑（ようすけ）／マイケル・マクドウェル

監修者

田地野（たじの） 彰（あきら）

発行者

小田 実紀

発行所

株式会社Clover出版

〒162-0843 東京都新宿区市谷田町3-6 THE GATE ICHIGAYA 10階　Tel.03(6279)1912　Fax.03(6279)1913

http://cloverpub.jp

印刷所

日経印刷株式会社

©Yosuke Ishii／Michael McDowell 2020, Printed in Japan

ISBN978-4-908033-72-8　C0082

乱丁、落丁本はお手数ですが 小社までお送りください。送料当社負担にてお取り替えいたします。

本書の内容の一部または全部を無断で複製、掲載、転載することを禁じます。

本書の内容に関するお問い合わせは、info@cloverpub.jp宛にメールでお願い申し上げます